# THE 2016 LINKEDIN GUIDE FOR FINANCIAL ADVISORS

*Six Steps to Identify Qualified Prospects
and Generate Referrals*

## BY CLAIRE AKIN, MBA

# ACKNOWLEDGEMENTS

I'm thankful to everyone who helped me create this book, especially:

My dog Wally, for your gentle snoring and patient company while I wrote.

My husband Josh, for your friendship, love and firm nudges to finish this project on time; you mean everything to me.

My friend and editor Melissa, for your insight, prose, and sunny optimism.

My Mom, for cheering me on with a nervous smile as I left my full-time job to start my own company.

My Dad, for introducing me to this business, supporting my career, and always telling me to put socks on when it's cold.

My brother and business coach Michael, for being my personal Tony Robbins.

My clients, for your ideas, enthusiasm, and collaboration.

# Introduction

I'm the type of person that has to believe in the "why" behind what I do every day. Before Simon Sinek spelled out the concept in his book, *Start with Why*, I spent a lot of time contemplating the importance of my work and wondering if I was helping or hurting the world.

During my first job after college as a buyer for Bumble Bee Foods, I worried about mercury levels in fish and depleting our oceans. Later, as a medical device marketing rep, I lost sleep over efficacy concerns in the devices I was selling. I actually worked for the Department of Defense for almost a year before I walked away from an interesting and high-paying job. It turns out the Department of Defense is also the Department of Offense, and I didn't want to spend my days buying parts for weapons.

I enjoyed many job functions I tried, including sales and working as an advisor. But marketing is my passion, it's what I am good at, what I love to do, and what I read about on the weekends for fun. Within my role as a marketer, I could probably work in different industries, but I have spent a lot of time thinking through which products I want to help push. Today, as a marketing consultant for independent financial advisors, I've never felt so good about my clients and the value I help them deliver.

## My Story

I grew up in the financial services industry. My dad has worked in the industry for over 37 years and became an independent advisor as soon as the idea came out in 1981. He has been affiliated with LPL Financial since we called it 'Linsco Private Ledger' and is currently their 7th longest tenured advisor. His brother and best friend are also both advisors in the same OSJ, so family gatherings include a lot of investment talk.

As soon as I got my driver's license at 16, I started working for my dad's firm after school. Once I got my MBA, I took over his marketing department and worked as an advisor myself. Today I still support his team, but I also work with a handful of advisors to run their marketing departments. Collaborating with this group of professionals is deeply rewarding and limitlessly fascinating. Here are a few reasons why I work with financial advisors:

## Advisors Are Entrepreneurs

Many of the advisors I work with have similar personalities — they're intelligent, analytical, extroverted, and driven. Could you think of a more interesting group of folks to work with every day? At their core, advisors are entrepreneurs who create and run businesses. This breeds passion, enthusiasm, and fresh ideas to consistently grow. As an entrepreneur myself, I admire and enjoy learning from the advisors I work with and collaborating with them.

## They Do Important Work

I get frustrated when I hear people talk about advisors as dishonest or greedy. It's unfair that large financial institutions and Wall Street brokers have given everyday advisors a bad rap. Even Tony Robbins has been badmouthing advisors recently, apparently not understanding the difference between brokers and independent advisors.

The advisors I work with spend long hours helping their clients and work even harder to make sure their advice is honest and unbiased. Independent advisors are educators, helping people understand the options available to them and make confident decisions. They help folks save for retirement, create financial security, plan for their children's education, and give to the causes they care about. Our communities and futures are better as a result.

## They're Members of Our Communities

Growing up with the last name *Dobransky* and a father who is 6'7" tall, I ran into a lot of people who knew my dad in our town. I can't recall the number of times someone told me what a great guy my dad is, or how he had helped them, or how much they appreciate his work.

When my brother and his friend's played Little League, even when times were tight and markets were down, my dad's firm would always pay for the uniforms and team events. I also remember many days when I saw my dad don his black suit and go to a funeral for a client, a neighbor, or a community member.

Advisors are important members of our communities, helping us save for the future and supporting our friends and neighbors. Most advisors I know give back to their communities, whether raising money for local charities or educating community members on financial topics. More than any other financial services or professional group, I see advisors giving back to their communities.

## They're Good People

My first job out of graduate school was in the fast-paced world of medical device sales, touring the country and attending swanky conferences with no FINRA limits on non-cash compensation. On more than one occasion, I saw a sales rep slip off their wedding band as they entered a conference cocktail party, which was disheartening, to say the least.

Despite the reputation that our industry has for greed and corruption, the advisors I know are the most honest, integrous people you will meet. I love attending broker-dealer conferences and seeing the same advisors year after year with their spouses and children. We're part of a lovely group of people who work hard and do the right thing for their clients and their families.

## They Help People

During my childhood, I was alarmed a few times when we came home to tearful messages on our answering machine from a client whose spouse had died. At first, I worried that my dad's clients were dying off and there would soon be none left. But over the years, I noticed that he was often the first person they called when tragedy struck.

People always list doctors, lawyers, and accountants in the same category as financial advisors in terms of the role they play in clients' lives. But could you imagine calling your doctor or lawyer to lean on during a divorce or death? Client meetings can feel like therapy sessions at times and some advisors I know are trained in crisis counseling. The role advisors play in client lives is much more than financial.

Last week I was on the phone with an advisor I work with who was driving home 100 miles after helping an elderly client move into a retirement home. Another advisor was running late to lunch because he had been helping his client shop for a new car. My dad is always accompanying his elderly clients to make big decisions or move furniture. To have someone trusted to call during times of need is a meaningful and important benefit.

If you are an advisor, I appreciate all that you do to serve your clients and your community. I am happy to support you in providing valuable and significant work. While you work hard and shoulder tremendous responsibility, the skeptics question your integrity and compliance never cuts you a break. It may not be easy, but the work you do sure is important.

## Why I Wrote This Book

I got the idea to write this book after years of answering questions from advisors looking for help with LinkedIn. After explaining the same concepts over and over, one advisor said, "You should write a book on this stuff."

My goal is to inspire you to stop being confused, intimidated, or frustrated by LinkedIn. It's not rocket science and it only takes a small upfront investment of time to master. The lingo and interface can be downright annoying to use and I am the first to admit it isn't always user-friendly. But that's no excuse to give up.

If you are an advisor, I guarantee that you deal with more difficult and technical systems every day to research investments, rebalance accounts, and create financial plans. The difference is that you've given yourself permission to be an expert in those arenas. Trust me when I tell you that you're capable of navigating all of the complexities LinkedIn has to offer if you put forth some determination and a little patience. If you approach the effort with a can-do attitude, it will be a piece of cake.

That said, my own Dad still will not log in to his LinkedIn profile unless I am physically sitting next to him. He forwards me the email notifications from LinkedIn and asks me to come to his office and help him log on. Luckily, my office is less than a mile from his, so I agree to show up if he'll make coffee. It's perfectly fine to ask your kids, spouse, or administrative assistant for help until you feel more confident.

However, if you get one thing from this book, I hope you empower yourself to figure this stuff out on your own. Our world has gotten more techy in the past decade, but it is also easier than ever to find good tutorials online. Every time you get stuck, Google what you're trying to accomplish for instructions or watch a YouTube video on the process. No matter the topic, I promise there's help on the Internet.

As a Millennial, I get pushback from advisors that I don't understand how difficult all this social media stuff is for them, and I understand that. But I am actually in the older wave of the Millennial generation; Facebook didn't come out until I was almost through college.

My younger Millennial siblings think I am older than dirt and I don't "get" their social media practices. They laugh when I use emoticons "wrong" or don't know what their trendy new acronyms mean. My two younger sisters-in-law are not only done using Facebook, they're already "so over" Instagram!

Snapchat is all the range with that age group, and since I want to be involved in their lives (and let's face it; I want to seem cool) I'm in the process of learning how to be the savviest of all Snapchatters. All it takes is 30 minutes of time, some focus, and a couple YouTube videos. I'll have my finger on the pulse of their lives until they take up some new social network next month.

I sincerely hope this book is helpful in bringing you up to speed on LinkedIn and I wish you best of luck in your marketing and your business. Thanks for all that you do for your clients and your community!

# What is LinkedIn and Why Do I Need It?

Whe I give my presentation, "How to Use LinkedIn to Generate Referrals" at national broker-dealer conferences, financial advisors often remark that the practices I teach are the same they've been using for years. One advisor commented that his life insurance sales process in the late 1970's involved using a neighborhood phone book before each sales meeting with prospects to identify three of their neighbors to ask for an introduction.

He would show up at the home of the client or prospect and give his sales presentation, then ask them how well they knew their neighbors on his list. Based on their response, he would either ask for an introduction or ask whether they knew another set of neighbors better. Once they agreed to make an introduction, he would give his presentation to the neighbors and prepare a list of three more families to ask for introductions.

This advisor found this process to be successful, even with the obvious drawback that it was impossible to target prospects in a sophisticated way based on their address. I teach advisors to follow the same process online using LinkedIn, but to identify highly-qualified prospects to ask for an introduction.

With LinkedIn prospecting, you are able to target individuals based on specific variables such as the company they work for, the position they hold, shared interests, alma mater, age, location, gender, charitable causes, prior employers, and more. The more precise you can be in qualifying the prospects you can offer the most value for, the more effective and efficient your prospecting will become.

The networking fundamentals that worked in the past still work today and are much easier and less time-consuming to employ using LinkedIn as a tool. The strategies you will learn in this book will allow you to employ LinkedIn in a way that makes sense for your specific business. We'll review various strategies and give plenty of examples to reach your target audience, stand out from the crowd, and attract valuable leads.

# What is LinkedIn?

In short, LinkedIn is a business-oriented social networking platform. But before you lump LinkedIn into the "social media" category, I want you to understand that the platform is not what you may traditionally consider social media. There are no cat videos or family photos, nor do you need to be savvy with emoticons and social media lingo to effectively use the platform. LinkedIn is simply a tool that allows you to execute tried and true networking practices more efficiently and intelligently.

There are four main categories that LinkedIn is used for worldwide, which are in order of prevalence:

- Job Seeking

- Recruiting

- Sales

- Networking

While the LinkedIn revenue model is based around Job Seeking and Recruiting, the benefit for financial advisors is in the networking capabilities. LinkedIn offers four main uses for advisors:

1. It's your online resume

2. It's an online rolodex of your network

3. It's a powerful search tool to find and connect with qualified prospects

4. It's a publishing platform that allows you to share your expertise

**The Problem that LinkedIn Solves**

Remember the old days when you would exchange business cards with a contact at a networking event or on the golf course so that you could refer business to one another in the future? The problem with that practice is that once your contact changed companies, the business card was rendered useless. Because workers change jobs more often today than they did years ago, this problem has been magnified.

LinkedIn offers a solution to this problem, allowing you to virtually exchange business cards and stay in touch no matter the career transitions that you or your connection make. In fact, LinkedIn will let you know each time one of your connections changes companies so you can reach out and congratulate them, keep in touch, and perhaps ask if they have rolled over their old 401(k). By connecting with your network on LinkedIn, you can stay in touch, grow your network, share your expertise, and ask for introductions.

# A Brief History of the Online Networking Tool

LinkedIn was started by a group of Silicon Valley entrepreneurs, including a few Paypal alums, in early 2003 as a business networking tool. They first toyed with the name "Colleaguester" but later settled on "LinkedIn." When the platform was launched, there were just 10 members. Growth was slow at first, with only 20 new members per day at times, but the idea attracted investment from Sequoia Capital in the fall of 2003.

The founding idea was *"If you have 20 trusted business contacts and they each have 20 of their own contacts, you could potentially contact 150,000 business professionals through a network you already know and trust."*

In some ways, LinkedIn was an antidote to the impersonalization the Internet brought to business. In a sea of new websites and online searches, professionals still wanted to do business with those they already had a trusted relationship with. LinkedIn allowed them to connect online to refer business and find qualified job candidates.

Growth exploded in 2004 when the platform allowed members to upload their email address book and connect with their contacts in bulk. In 2005, the platform emerged as the top resource for job seekers and recruiters, which it remains today. During 2006, the company achieved profitability mainly through recruiting services, and membership topped 5 million.

*Yahoo!* executive Jeff Weiner took over as CEO in 2009 and the company went public in 2011 with 100 million members.

Once LinkedIn had reached a "network effect" as the de facto online professional platform, it quickly spread globally and today has offices in Omaha, Chicago, Los Angeles, New York, San Francisco, Washington, London, Dublin, Amsterdam, Milan, Munich, Madrid, Stockholm, Singapore, Hong Kong, China, Japan, Australia, Canada, India and Dubai.

There are now over 400 million users in 200 countries, with over 111 million users in the United States. LinkedIn.com is the 14th most visited website in the world on a daily basis. Still widely used by job seekers and recruiters, LinkedIn more recently has become a publishing, messaging and news sharing platform.

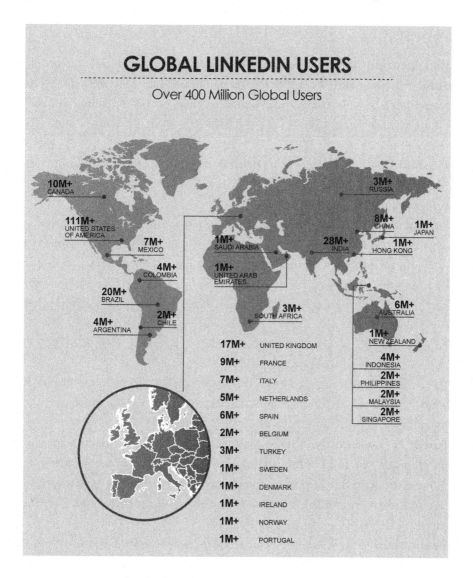

GLOBAL LINKEDIN USERS

Over 400 Million Global Users

## Anatomy of LinkedIn

If you aren't currently on LinkedIn, a good starting point is to understand the basics. If you are on LinkedIn, you may find that it changes so often that a review of terminology is helpful.

## Your Profile

Your LinkedIn profile serves as your online resume. You create a profile using your name and email address. Then, you add information such as your photo, job title, education, and experience. There are several main parts of a profile including:

**Headline:** Your headline appears just under your name and should include what you do and who you serve. This is searchable by keyword and must be 120 characters or less.

**Summary:** This 2,000 character summary of your expertise and experience is also searchable by Google to help people find you, both from the LinkedIn internal search function and from a Google search. You should use this space to showcase a brief bio and explain your specialties. It's important to note that you can upload videos, blog posts, and websites to your summary.

**Experience:** The experience section is similar to a resume where you list former employers and work experience.

**Education:** Similar to a resume, the education section of your profile is where you list which schools you attended, the degrees you earned, and any organizations you were involved in.

**Posts:** The LinkedIn publishing platform is essentially a blog within your profile where you can publish original content and share with your network. These articles are different than updates because all of your connections are notified when you publish a post and your posts permanently reside on your profile.

**Publications:** This is where you list books you have authored or relevant publications.

**Certifications:** Include any licenses or credentials here such as CFP®, AIF®, and securities licenses.

**Recommendations:** Recommendations are text comments similar to a letter of recommendation that is featured permanently on your profile. They are helpful for job seekers. FINRA does not allow recommendations because they could be seen as testimonials.

**Endorsements:** This feature allows your first degree connections to "endorse" you for a skill with just one click. They are searchable by skill and are also helpful for job seekers and recruiters. Most large broker-dealers do not allow endorsements.

## Your Network

**Your 1st Degree Connections:** These are individuals you are connected with on LinkedIn, similar to "friends" on Facebook. You can message these connections directly and view their profiles.

**Your 2nd Degree Connections:** The connections of your connections are your 2nd degree connections. You can view more of their profile than someone who you are not connected with and you may request to connect with them directly. You can also search these connections and ask for an introduction to third degree and out of network contacts.

**Group Members:** People who belong to the same LinkedIn groups are considered part of your network. You are able to send a message to them directly using the group message feature.

## Advanced Search

The advanced search function allows you to search LinkedIn's member database to find prospects or people you'd like to connect with. The search criteria are vast, including job title (past or present), keyword, seniority level, postal code, company, etc. We'll review this tool in detail later in the book.

## Sponsored Posts

These ads are posts that have been sponsored to show up in the activity feed of their targeted prospects. You can create a sponsored post to show up in the activity feed for a group of prospects, such as Engineering CEOs within 10 miles of your office.

## Company Page

A LinkedIn Company Page is a profile for your business. You can share company information, products, and news on this page and individuals may follow updates from your page directly.

## Company Page Followers

LinkedIn users that click "follow" on your company page recieve updates in their activity feed when you post to that page.

## Inbox

Your LinkedIn inbox is where you can send, view, and receive LinkedIn messages. The messaging feature must be captured by compliance archiving software and may not be approved, so check with your compliance department before using this feature.

## InMail

InMail messages are LinkedIn emails that you can send directly to any LinkedIn member, from Janet Yellen to Bill Gates, even if you're not connected. You can purchase InMail credits and they are only redeemed if you get a response.

## LinkedIn Message

LinkedIn messages are free to your first degree connections and fellow group members. This is a cost effective and quick way to reach out to your network. The messaging feature must be captured by compliance archiving software and may not be approved, so check with your compliance department before using this feature.

## Mention

You can mention a person or a company page in an update. They are automatically notified that you have mentioned them in your status.

## LinkedIn Groups

LinkedIn Groups provide a place for professionals in the same industry or with similar interests to share content, ask questions, and post jobs. I recommend joining groups where your prospects reside and sharing content valuable content within the groups.

## Group Announcement

A group announcement is sent to the email inbox of every member of the group. They can only be sent every 7 days and must be sent by a group administrator.

## LinkedIn Influencer

LinkedIn Influencer is the designation given to approximately 500 professionals who were invited to publish on LinkedIn before the publishing platform was opened up to all members. The list includes Richard Branson, Bill Gates, Arianna Huffington, and David Cameron.

## LinkedIn Pulse

The LinkedIn Pulse app was built as a class project at Stanford University in 2010 with a goal of delivering custom news tailored to you based on your network. With pulse, you get custom activity feeds based on what is trending among your connections.

# Who is On LinkedIn?

One of the common misconceptions I hear from financial advisors is, "Because I'm over 50, my clients and prospects are not on LinkedIn." However, I know from working with hundreds of advisors that when I upload their email address books to LinkedIn, over half of their clients typically have LinkedIn profiles set up and active.

If you think your prospects are not on LinkedIn, consider that one in three professionals worldwide have profiles and LinkedIn networking strategies are a mainstay at all of the top U.S. business schools. Pew Research Center surveys show that the average user is 44 years old, their average income is $109,000, and their average investable asset value is over $250,000. If your new client account minimum is above $250,000, consider that 26% of ultra-high net-worth investors also use LinkedIn. As the Great Transfer of Wealth begins, LinkedIn is becoming more important for your legacy plan, with the fastest growing segment being Millennials.

The higher average income of users and professional culture of the network make it an ideal social network for financial advisors. It is the only major social network where more users today are in the 30-64 age range than the 18-29 range.

- 31% of adults 30–49 use LinkedIn.

- 30% of adults 50–64 use LinkedIn.

- 23% of adults 18–29 use LinkedIn.

- 21% of adults over 65 use LinkedIn.

The platform also caters to relatively educated users:

- 50% of adult college graduates use LinkedIn.

- 22% of adults with some college experience use LinkedIn.

- 12% of adults with high school or less experience use LinkedIn.

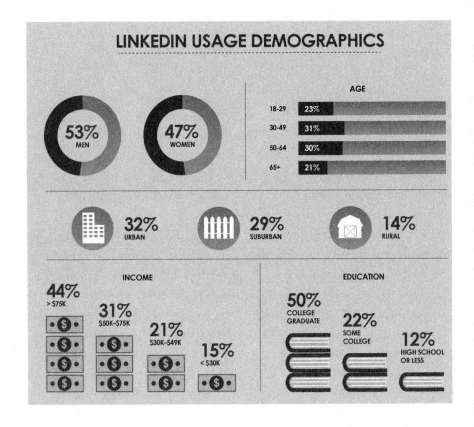

## Why Not Facebook or Twitter?

While other social media platforms have higher membership rates and see more daily traffic, there is more content to compete with. Over 58% of the entire U.S. adult population is on Facebook and the average user spends 405 minutes per month on the site, according to the Wall Street Journal.

However, most users actively share their own content, which creates significant noise to compete with. By contrast, only 10% of LinkedIn users generate over 80% of the content. If you are active on LinkedIn, you can stand out from the crowd and gain significant exposure in an arena where users are seeking business and financial news.

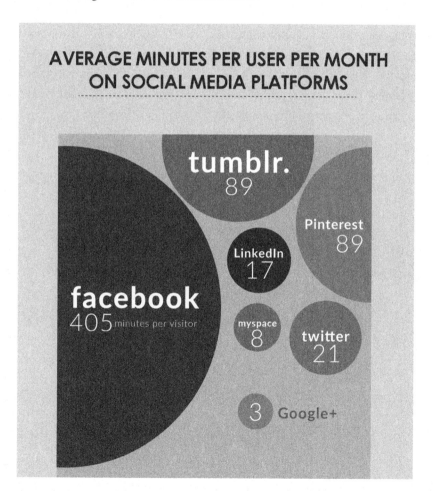

# How Can LinkedIn Help Me?

You may have heard that LinkedIn is important for your professional image and for targeting younger prospects like Millennials. But can it help you to increase AUM for your current target market? Research suggests that using LinkedIn helps advisors prospect new leads within their niche and also supports their existing referral process.

While the financial services industry got a late start with social media due to compliance fears, most large institutions have caught on to the benefits of LinkedIn. Every major independent broker-dealer has now approved the use of LinkedIn with a few compliance precautions.

Today, 7 out of 10 financial advisors are using social media for marketing, according to a study conducted by FTI Consulting. Of those advisors, 90% use LinkedIn as their primary platform. Of the advisors using LinkedIn, 60% who use the techniques we'll review for client prospecting gained new clients as a result. One third of these advisors generated $1 million or more in assets under management through their efforts.

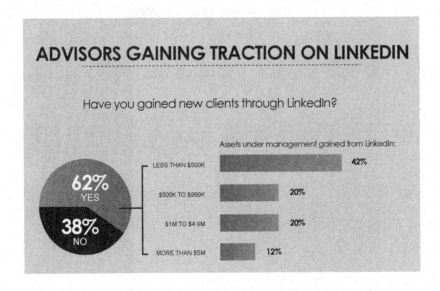

*Data Credit: FTI Consulting.*

While studies and research indicate that advisors are using LinkedIn successfully, what about in real life? In my work helping advisors with their marketing, we find that about 30% of traffic to their website comes from their activity on LinkedIn. This traffic is made up of over 50% of new prospects, meaning individuals who they do not already have a relationship with. When it comes to generating new leads, I have found LinkedIn to be more powerful and cost effective than any other channel including paid advertising, direct mail, seminars, and search engine optimization.

What is harder to directly quantify is how well LinkedIn helps support your existing referral process. We know that 9 out of 10 investors who are referred to an advisor by a friend or a family member will type the advisor's name into Google before they make an appointment. Google gives preferential treatment to LinkedIn profiles when returning search results. For this reason, if you Google your name, your LinkedIn profile is as likely to come up as your website. By having an up-to-date LinkedIn profile, you help prospects find you online, see who you are connected to, and feel more confident placing their trust in your firm.

### Case Studies of Average Advisors

I work with advisors to create, optimize, and run their LinkedIn marketing strategies. Often, I bring on new clients who have no prior LinkedIn exposure. While a marketing strategy using LinkedIn takes 6-12 months to mature, you can track the indicators of success below to guide your efforts and evaluate whether you are a beginner, intermediate, or advanced user.

With an average advisor, which I consider to be 55-60 years old with 20 years of experience, I find the following initial success within 30 days of beginning their LinkedIn strategy:

- 500+ LinkedIn Connections

- 10+ profile views per week

- 50 views per publication

With an intermediate LinkedIn user that employs the strategies I teach over 6 months or more, I expect to see a larger network and more activity including:

- 1000+ LinkedIn Connections

- 30+ profile views per week
- 100+ views per publication

With an advisor who has been actively using LinkedIn for more than one year and employing the strategies in this book, I expect to see significant success including:

- 2,000+ LinkedIn Connections
- 75+ profile views per week
- 300+ views per publication

By working to grow your network and visibility, each post and publication you share will garner more exposure and attract the attention of more leads and prospects. Over time, you will create an awareness as the subject matter expert in your field and stay top of mind with your network.

If you aren't yet an intermediate or advanced LinkedIn user, take heart in knowing that under utilizing LinkedIn is very common. The average CEO on LinkedIn has just 930 connections. Setting up a great looking profile is only half the battle, it's important to take steps to connect with your network, expand your reach, join groups, and share content. We'll review exactly how to do this in the following chapters.

## What is the Point?

Your objective for using LinkedIn will vary depending on your overall marketing goals. For most advisors, the objective is to increase assets under management. However, other goals include gaining exposure as an author or speaker, attracting talent, or finding acquisition targets.

Luckily, for most of the common objectives, the path to success is similar. No matter your goals, the value of your network on LinkedIn depends on three things: the quantity, quality, and strength of your connections. If you have a small group of connections who are executives at the largest employer in your city and are actively engaged with the content you post, your network is valuable. If you have a thousands of connections from various industries who you've never met, you will not be able to acquire introductions that pay off.

To increase the quantity, quality, and strength of your connections, we will review strategies that aim to do the following:

**Expand Your Network** by attracting prospects, joining groups where you interests overlap with the interests of those you'd like to meet, and aligning with key influencers.

**Engage With Your Connections** to deepen your relationships by giving feedback, communicating regularly, sharing relevant content with individuals, and reading what your connections are posting.

**Stay Top of Mind** by creating and sharing information that your connections are likely to find valuable. Through your content, remind people what you do and who you serve so that even those who are not clients can still recommend you.

By investing in your online network, you can grow your influence and support your referral process. Because LinkedIn is now anchored into our business culture, this investment will stay with you throughout your career and continue to pay dividends. Think of LinkedIn not as a social media platform, but as a tool to support and grow the relationships you've taken the time to build during your career.

The next chapter will present everything you need to know to create an outstanding LinkedIn profile on your own. But before we dive into the details, let's address the elephant in the room. If you are not on social media yet, what is holding you back?

# Are You Making a Mountain Out of Joining Social Media?

If there is one thing I encounter over and over with the advisors I work with, it's their too-strong-for-reason resistance to try out social media. We know that about one third of financial advisors are still not actively embracing social media. It's clear that advisors who do use social media enjoy faster and easier communication with clients, increased referral sources, and higher client retention.

A social media presence has been proven to be an important piece of an effective marketing plan, yet so many advisors are reluctant to take the plunge. Why is there still a strong opposition? Here are my top theories for why almost half of advisors are still not using social media. If you have not taken the plunge, consider whether you're letting one of these reasons hold you back.

## No Instant Gratification

We all love instant gratification. That's why we gamble (even though we know we're likely placing a losing bet) and eat that second scoop of ice cream. It's tough to stick to a plan that doesn't pay off right away. But as the Latin phrase "gutta cavat lapidem" or "a water drop hollows a stone" describes, progress is sometimes made not by force but by small actions repeated often.

Social media pays off at its own pace, but when it does, it tends to be significant. An advisor who I work with in San Diego had been using social media for five months with no results, until a former college sorority sister Facebook messaged her that she had just inherited $2 million from her grandmother. The payoff might be delayed and unpredictable, but you can't afford to miss out. I ask the advisors I work with to give an honest try for six months before they even think about giving up.

## It's Confusing

The digital age has changed our lives at an alarming rate and those of us who don't consider ourselves "tech savvy" have had a hard time keeping up. Social media and its terminology can be confusing, overwhelming and downright annoying. But the concepts behind the language are actually very simple. LinkedIn is a place to connect with professionals. Twitter is a place to share content. Facebook is a place to connect with friends. YouTube is a place to share videos. I assure you that in your financial advisory practice, you use much more complex technologies on a daily basis.

If you don't "get" social media yet, the best way to understand is to try it out by spending some time on the most popular sites. There is a good reason social media websites dominate traffic on the Internet; they're fun and interesting to use. Enlist your tech-savvy spouse, child, or friend to sit next to you and explain the basics, then explore at your own pace to find out what all the hype is about.

## Compliance Fears

The most common explanation (or excuse) I hear from advisors is that compliance regulations keep them from joining social media. Sure, compliance can be a burden, but the same rules apply whether you are writing a letter to clients, creating collateral for a seminar, or posting to social media. You must follow basic guidelines and avoid promissory statements. Broker-dealer firms have come a long way in recent years to support advisors use of social media and have made the process easier than ever.

The trick is to understand that the nature of social media marketing is not to make specific recommendations, but to offer general information and educational articles to connect with your network. Compliance will never stand in your way of using social media to achieve these results. In my work with advisors, I submit hundreds of articles per month for advisors to post on LinkedIn. On average, I see one or two required changes from compliance. The more you write and post, the easier the process gets.

## It Takes Too Much Time

Having a polished, professional and engaging social media presence does take some time. But the truth is that your social media efforts can and should coincide with the work you put into being a great advisor. All good advisors read interesting articles, watch educational videos or webinars, and come across compelling data.

If you take a few extra moments to share this information with your network, you will have a great social media presence. Whether you come across a change in Social Security, an interesting data point, or a local charity golf tournament, clients appreciate hearing from you. Invest a few extra minutes to post content you already consume and you will engage clients and prospects in a new way.

## The Cost

To be fair, there are often monetary costs associated with social media and compliance mechanisms to track them. However, these costs are relatively small and generally decreasing as broker-dealers continue to recognize the importance of social media marketing for advisors. To minimize the cost, I recommend focusing on LinkedIn only at first, which will run $60-80 per year for archiving software.

It's important to look at these costs as a fraction of your total marketing budget, similar to the postage for a direct mail campaign. If you get one new client or 10 good ideas from the endeavor, those investments have a positive ROI. Envision the cost as an investment in future business and let it be a motivator to regularly use your social media accounts.

Are you ready to employ LinkedIn to grow your business? If there is any doubt in your mind that you'll follow through on this process, turn to the next chapter and follow the steps for "How to Get Started on LinkedIn in One Hour." Once you get a basic profile up and running, there's no turning back. Already have a profile? Follow the steps in the next chapter to optimize your LinkedIn Profile, which acts as the hub of your LinkedIn marketing efforts.

# CHAPTER 2

# Getting Started on a Phenomenal Profile

Whether you are new to LinkedIn or have been using it for years, it's worthwhile to put in place strong fundamentals for your profile. As we discussed in the last chapter, your profile represents your professional image and will stay with you throughout your career. The investment towards making it great will pay off for years to come.

Unlike Facebook or Twitter, LinkedIn profiles are actually incredibly robust and take considerable time to set up. The average financial advisor spends over 6 hours setting up their LinkedIn profile. There are a few reasons for this. First, the platform is not intuitive for a first time user and can be frustrating to use. Second, most advisors get hung up writing their bio. It's difficult to write about oneself, especially if you are not used to writing in the style of a professional bio.

I recommend paying a professional service to set up your profile the first time to be sure it's done right and to save you time and energy. Your time is better spent adding the finishing touches to make your profile outstanding and using LinkedIn to network. There are plenty of companies out there, including my own, that charge about $200 to write your bio and optimize your profile.

# Can You Afford Not to Have a Great Profile?

Imagine your favorite client just referred one of their closest friends to your firm. However, since this A+ prospect is only armed with your name, not the URL of your website, they type your name into Google to learn more about you. As is common, instead of your website coming up, your LinkedIn profile is the top result. Are you comfortable with this first impression?

The reality is that keyword searches are often directed to LinkedIn due to the relevance that Google lends to LinkedIn profiles. Take a moment right now to Google your name and title. I am willing to bet that if you have a LinkedIn profile, it comes up above your website. So many advisors put time and money into their websites, then neglect to update their LinkedIn profiles.

The truth is, if you aren't using social media, your absence may be hurting your credibility. What's worse than not being on social media is having an incomplete or outdated profile. If you have been using one of the excuses above to put off creating your LinkedIn profile, commit yourself to spend one hour today to make it happen!

# How to Get Started on LinkedIn in One Hour

Creating an awesome LinkedIn profile that will impress for a lifetime takes hours. But you can come up with a B+ profile to create a nice presence in less than sixty minutes. This way, your absence will not hurt your credibility and you'll have a strong foundation to build upon.

Here are the simple steps to get started in one hour. Set a timer and challenge yourself to get the steps done on time. Once you've completed this exercise, we'll dig deeper into exactly how to build on the base you've created to make your profile outstanding.

## 1. Create Your Account (3 minutes)

Go to LinkedIn.com and click on "Join Today." Enter your first name, last name, email address, and password, then click "Join Now." Locate the verification email that LinkedIn sends automatically and click on the link to verify your account.

## 2. Craft a Keyword-Rich Summary (15 mins)

Don't worry about adding work experience or uploading your resume yet. The most important part of your profile is your summary, so start there. A good place to begin in writing your summary is the "About" section of your website.

You or someone in your firm likely has already invested some thought into this endeavor. Copy and paste the text from that page into your word processor, then make sure the details are up to date. Set a timer for 10 minutes and do the following:

- Don't try to reinvent the wheel and avoid writer's block caused by perfectionism. Just focus on getting a strong profile written by borrowing from existing sources of information.

- Answer in the simplest terms, what you do and who you do it for. List your ideal clients and the locations that you serve so that your profile will come up for keyword searches including these terms.

- Explain what makes your firm different in the same way you would answer at a cocktail party — short and to the point.

- Add a paragraph or two from your bio to explain your relevant credentials and experience.

Once you have a good rough draft, take a couple of minutes to tie the words together and run a spell check. Then, cut and paste into your summary section and click "Save."

## 3. Enter Your Contact Information (5 minutes)

Always direct traffic back to your website by listing your site's URL in the "Website" section of your profile under "Contact Info." Be sure to list your email and phone number so your connections can reach you. Add your Twitter profile, if applicable, for cross-pollination and to give your profile an SEO boost. Most broker-dealers will require that you hyperlink to FIRNA.org and SIPC.org, so save yourself a step and add those to the website section as well.

## 4. Upload a Headshot (2 mins)

Right click on your photo from your website and save it to your desktop. Then, upload and use the built-in LinkedIn photo editing tool to crop from the shoulders up. Profiles with photos get 13 times more views, so this step is essential.

## 5. Enter Education and Work Experience (10 mins)

1.  Click "Add Education," select your college and degree, and enter your graduation dates. List any extracurricular activities or honors. If you have a post-graduate degree, repeat the process.

2.  Click "Add Position" and list your three most relevant roles. Don't worry about listing that job from high school; this isn't a background check, it's simply a way to highlight your experience and the positions you're most proud of.

## 6. Join Three LinkedIn Groups (5 mins)

Think about your hobbies and interests. Then think about your ideal clients' hobbies and interests. Join three groups where there is overlap. This is how you can interact with prospects you don't already have a relationship with, but may fit into your firm's model.

To search for groups, type a keyword into the main search bar at the very top of LinkedIn and press enter. Once the results are displayed, look over on the left side and click on "Groups" to display all of the groups that fit this keyword. In a search for "Equestrian," LinkedIn returns groups for Professional Equestrians, Equestrian Enthusiasts, Real Estate Equestrians, Equestrian Business Owners, and more. Try a few searches and join at least three groups. Don't forget to search for your town or neighborhood and join local groups.

## 7. Connect with Your Network (15 mins)

LinkedIn makes it easy to upload your email contacts and connect with all clients and prospects. Don't be shy! Most folks are happy to receive an invitation and expand their network. Be sure to add the email addresses for centers of influence, such as CPAs and attorneys, with whom you work.

On the top of the page, click on "Connections," and then "Add Connections." Use the built-in interface to integrate with your email server such as Outlook. You can also upload a .CSV file of your email addresses. Navigate to your email system, go to "Contacts," and click "Export." If you export as an Excel Spreadsheet, you can open the spreadsheet and convert it to a .CSV file, typically under File - Export To. If you get stuck, Google the instructions for your particular email system, as there are often good step-by-step instructions online.

## 8. Submit to Compliance and Celebrate (5 mins)

To export your profile and submit to compliance, click on Profile on the top navigation. Once you are viewing your own profile, there's a button that reads "View Profile As." Just to the right of that button is a carrot drop down menu. The fourth option is "Save to PDF." This will automatically download a PDF of your profile that you can submit to compliance. If you completed the process on time, pat yourself on the back and move on!

# SEO and LinkedIn

When writing your headline and designing your profile, it's helpful to understand the keyword SEO hierarchy LinkedIn uses. SEO is short for search engine optimization and it refers to the process by which search engines choose which results to return for a given keyword search.

For LinkedIn, keyword searches give the most search weight to your name, then your headline, and then your job title. Following is your summary, experience, and skills. It's important to structure the keywords in your profile appropriately with disproportionate consideration given to the keywords in your headline.

However, that's not the end of the story. If someone does a search that matches your name and headline word-for-word, your profile may not come up first. That's because LinkedIn uses a Google-like algorithm to attempt to return the most relevant search results first. They give weight to profiles using the following factors:

- Average weekly profile views (how popular your profile is)
- How complete your profile is
- The websites listed in your "Contact Info"
- Whether you have a custom URL (more on this later)
- How many connections you have
- How many connections your connections have
- How many high ranking profiles you are connected to
- How often people click on your profile from a search
- How many groups you belong to
- How active you are on LinkedIn and within groups
- Multimedia content on your profile (more on this later, too)
- Backlinks to your profile (listing your LinkedIn profile on your website and other social sites)

Although most of these are not easily affected, it's helpful to keep them in mind when executing your overall strategy to build your profile, network, and activity.

## Writing Your Profile

Now that your LinkedIn profile exists, you'll want to spend some time thoughtfully articulating who you are and what you do. Let's begin with the sections you'll need to write:

- Your headline
- Your summary
- Your experience

## Your Headline

LinkedIn Headlines are 120 character "hooks" that appear right under your name on your profile and in search results. Similar to a newspaper or magazine headline, it should be catchy, interesting, and easy to read. Your headline is your opportunity to capture interest and invite users to learn more about you.

Many LinkedIn experts will tell you that your headline is the most important part of your profile, and this may be true for job seekers. However, for financial advisors, I disagree. I find that a profile summary section that resonates with prospects is more impactful than a great headline. Since advisors depend much more heavily on referrals, most keyword searches will be for the advisor's name or firm name.

You may not realize that headlines show up with your name during an active search, meaning as I am typing into the LinkedIn search bar, profiles and their corresponding headlines appear under my search. Because your entire headline appears during a search, it has an impact on whether people choose to click on your profile and learn more about you.

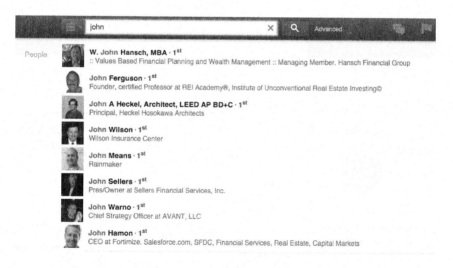

## Awful Headlines

Despite their importance, most LinkedIn headlines are abysmal. The majority of LinkedIn users do not understand what a headline should be or its impact. Most people list their job title or company and fail to take advantage of all 120 characters.

Marketing in general should always focus on how you can benefit prospects. Unfortunately, people do not care about what you do, they care about how you may be able to help them. Some of the worst headlines I see highlight what an advisor does, how he thinks he is great, how he views himself, but nothing regarding the benefit he could offer prospects.

Just for fun, let's take a look at some real life terrible headlines:

**"I love selling life insurance!"** What does this have to do with me, the prospective buyer? Just because you love doing something doesn't make you good at it. Who do you sell life insurance to? What types do you specialize in? How are you different than every other life insurance salesperson?

**"Rainmaker"** For who? In which industry? What are you selling? If I am a prospective buyer, I may be put on the defensive by the headline, as I'm not sure I want you rainmaking with my money.

**"President at Jones, Inc."** While this may be your title and company, it tells me nothing about who you serve, what your firm does, what you do, or how I can benefit. Unfortunately, this is the most common headline I see for advisors.

**"Author, Speaker, Life Coach & Veterinary Pharmaceutical Sales"** This may be my favorite. I'm sorry, but you cannot possibly be the best of the best at each of these endeavors. Too many titles and keywords can be confusing to prospects. For your headline, choose your "main thing" and focus on it.

**"☆ Lead Generation - Roofing Contractors ☆ Contractor Marketing ☆ Author of Best-Selling 80/20 Internet Lead Generation ☆"** Please do not use symbols or emoticons. They come across as childish, cluttered, and unprofessional. Write your headline as a headline, which is a string of words that form a cohesive thought, not a hodgepodge of separate ideas and symbols.

**"Unix SME / IA SME / IAM at SPAWAR SSC PAC"** This is an actual headline for a government contractor in my network. His experience section reads only the following: *"TSw IA Lead, IAO for 5 TSw systems, TSw OCRS Coordinator, Unix SME, IAM for Piers renovation."* While his peers might understand what that means, it's best practice to translate your LinkedIn profile into language that a layperson can understand. For advisors, this means being careful about your designations and acronyms.

## How to Write a Great Headline

Headlines should give three important pieces of information as clearly as possible:

1. What You Do

2. Who You Do it For

3. How it Benefits *Them*

Of course, it is challenging to sum up your value in 120 characters. The more specialized and clear you can be, the better your ideal prospects will be able to find you. As you use LinkedIn regularly, you'll find yourself updating your headline periodically when you get a better idea or come up with a more elegant way of phrasing your value. Essentially, you should try to convey *the value you offer to your specific clients.*

Remember that headlines are searchable by keyword, so you'll want to spend some time thinking about what your prospects might type into a search when trying to find an advisor to help them with their particular plight. Terms like "Wealth Manager," "Financial Advisor," "Estate Planner" are more powerful than "Founder," "Managing Partner," or "CEO" from a keyword search perspective.

## Which Keywords Do Prospects Use to Search?

To better understand which keywords prospects may be searching for to locate your firm, you may want to take a look at your website's Google Analytics, which allows you to see the traffic to your website and where it came from.

Within Google Analytics, under the Acquisition - Overview - Organic Search section, you can see which keywords folks are searching for to find your website, and incorporate them into your headline and profile. These keywords are different for every business. Here are some real life keyword search terms for some of the advisors I work with:

- *Financial Advisor Glastonbury CT*

- *Thomas Dobransky LPL*

- *Financial Help Toledo*

- *Investment Planning for Women*

- *Charitable Remainder Trust Advisor*

- *Business Planning for Anesthesiologist*

## Should Job Title be Included?

Often, advisors ask me whether they should list their job title and firm name in their headline. Keep in mind that both your job title and your firm name will be listed in your "Experience" section, so there is no need to list them again in your headline, unless you have good reason to from an SEO perspective.

If you work for a very large firm with high name recognition, I would use the firm name in your headline, such as *Wealth Advisor at Carson Wealth Management Group.*

If your firm name has your own name in it, I would leave it out since that keyword is already accounted for in your name. If your firm name clearly states what you do and who you do it for, I would include the name, such as *Financial Advisor with Engaging Women in Wealth Financial Group.*

The bottom line is that if you have reason to believe prospects are searching for your business name and it is different from your actual name, include it in your headline. Likewise, if you have professional designations, add them to your name or headline, as some prospects include "CFP" or "CFA" in their search terms.

## The Trick to Showing Up for Keyword Searches

There's a really easy trick to help your profile show up for a given keyword search that is effective as of January 1st, 2016. LinkedIn's algorithm seems to give double weight to keywords that are present both in a headline and job title, whether past or present. So, if you would like to show up for a given keyword search, add the string of keywords to your headline and current job title.

For my profile, I aim to show up for "Marketing Consultant for Financial Advisors." When I listed the keywords in only my headline and my job title as "Marketing Consultant," I did not show up within the first page of search results. However, when I change my current and past job titles from "Marketing Consultant" to "Marketing Consultant for Financial Advisors," I became the top search result for that keyword search, even for users who are not connected to me.

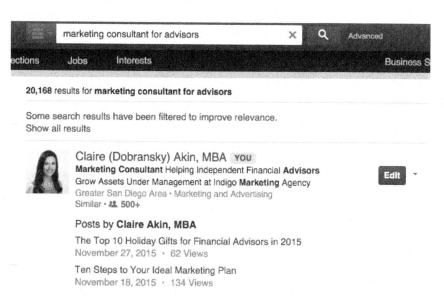

## Effective Headlines

The trick to writing a good headline is to balance the use of keywords for search engines and also write a headline that resonates with humans looking to learn more about how you can help them.

I know from Google Analytics that keyword searches for my own business website typically include "Claire Akin," "Indigo Marketing Agency", and "marketing consultant for financial advisors." I wrote my headline as "Marketing Consultant Helping Independent Financial Advisors Grow Assets Under Management at Indigo Marketing Agency." It is relevant-keyword-rich and explains exactly what I do, who I do it for, and how I help my clients.

Here are some examples of effective headlines for advisors:

- *Fee-only Financial Advisor Serving Widows and Divorcees at Haven Financial Solutions, Inc.*

- *Wealth Manager Serving Individuals and Biotech Businesses in San Diego, California*

- *Pension Consultant Specializing in Custom 401(k) and Defined Benefit Plan Design*

- *CERTIFIED FINANCIAL PLANNER™ for Entrepreneurial & Professional Women in Southern California*

- *Chartered Retirement Planning Counselor Providing Alternative Investment Advice to Accredited Investors*

- *Experienced Investment Advisor Offering Institutional Cash Management for School Districts in Texas*

# How to Write A Compelling Summary

Most advisors have trouble writing about themselves and the benefits they offer clients. Writing a LinkedIn summary is a combination of writing your own bio, creating a Wikipedia entry for yourself and your firm, and weaving in keywords. Because your summary is the most important part of your profile, prepare to dig deep to make it awesome.

## Step 1: What Are You?

Wikipedia, the online encyclopedia, has revolutionized the way we access knowledge. It has also changed the expectations of how information should be presented. Flooded by content and noise, we are all looking to understand the context of information quickly. Today's Internet users expect information to be communicated clearly, concisely, and within context. Take a look at how Wikipedia clearly explains the following concepts:

**LinkedIn** is a business-oriented social networking service. Founded in December 2002 and launched on May 5, 2003, it is mainly used for professional networking. As of October 2015, LinkedIn reports more than 400 million acquired users in more than 200 countries and territories.

**Modern portfolio theory (MPT)** is a theory of finance that attempts to maximize portfolio expected return for a given amount of risk, by carefully choosing the proportions of various assets. MPT is widely used in practice in the financial industry and several of its creators including Harry Markowitz won a Nobel memorial prize for the theory.

**A wormhole** is a hypothetical topological feature that would fundamentally be a shortcut connecting two separate points in spacetime. A wormhole, in theory, might be able to connect extremely far distances such as a billion light years or more, short distances such as a few feet, different universes, and different points in time.

The Wikipedia description style allows us to understand anything, no matter our familiarity of the subject, by reading a few simple sentences. The same should be true for your LinkedIn Summary. Someone with no knowledge of your industry, firm, or profession should be able to understand what you are by the first three sentences in your summary. Here are some examples:

*Claire Akin is an author, speaker, and marketing expert that helps independent financial advisors grow their firms through marketing. She runs Indigo Marketing Agency, a full service marketing firm serving top advisors, headquartered in San Diego. Claire is a former Investment Advisor Representative who holds her MBA in Marketing from the Rady School of Management at UC San Diego as well as a BA in Economics from UC Davis.*

*Todd Farmer is a pension consultant and the co-founder of Farmer & Betts Pension Consultants, a fee-based third party pension administration and consulting firm that does not offer investments or insurance. As a pension plan expert, he is driven by the belief that our private retirement plan system works. He and his brother, Tref Farmer, founded F&B Pension Consultants together with Miley Betts, with the goal of serving as trusted experts to offer custom retirement plans and third party administration.*

*Paul Loyacono is an investment manager and the founder of WealthPoint Investment Management, an independent financial planning firm dedicated to helping clients plan for retirement while investing with the goal of minimizing risk. Paul has more than a decade of experience in the financial services industry and is passionate about making a positive impact on his clients' lives. He works with a wide variety of clients, from millennials to retirees in Ridgeland, Madison, Jackson, Tupelo, the Delta and Vicksburg, Mississippi as well as throughout the South.*

## Step 2: Why Do Clients Choose You Over Competitors?

Dig deep and think about why your clients choose to work with you, rather than a competitor that offers similar services. Most advisors haven't thought through exactly why clients make the decision to work with them. It's helpful to ask some of your clients why they hired you and what they think makes you different. Is it your experience with their particular demographic? The investment philosophy you offer? Shared interests? More than likely, clients choose to work with you because of a service-related aspect, like the trust they have in you or the support they get from your staff.

Clients initially choose to take action and work with you to solve one of their problems. Try to understand which problem you are solving for your top clients. Do you simplify their financial picture? Do you offer risk management that helps them sleep at night? Do you educate them so they can make informed financial decisions and feel empowered? By understanding the biggest problem you solve for clients, you can more persuasively illustrate the benefits you offer to potential clients.

I recommend addressing what makes you different in your second paragraph of your summary. Here are a few angles we could take for the same advisor:

*Clients often choose to work with Paul because of his conservative and disciplined investment process. He understands that his clients worry about another financial crisis as they approach retirement. They find confidence in knowing that his firm uses a carefully structured process for choosing investments and aiming to minimize risk.*

*Retirees typically work with Paul because of his dedication to building trusted relationships and his conservative investment philosophy. Often, his clients approaching retirement want to work with a younger advisor who can see them both to and through their retirement. He understands their fears of outliving their retirement savings and works to help them feel confident in their financial plan.*

*Millennials frequently enjoy working with Paul due to his transparent fees and proactive communication. His team offers leading technology to allow clients to access their accounts from their mobile devices and view all of their financial information in one place.*

## Step 3: Weave a Story

I know from analyzing website visitor behavior from hundreds of advisors' sites that prospects first want to know what you do, then *why* you do it. Website visitors come to a homepage, then immediately click on "About Us" or "My Story."

The story is the most common missing thread in bios I read. Humans are social creatures and we relate to each other through stories. We also perceive more value in objects if we attribute an interesting story to an item. It is for this reason that great works of art can be worth millions and conversation pieces in a home create interest.

Consider *The Significant Object Project*, an experiment that set out to prove the hypothesis "Narrative transforms insignificant objects into significant ones." The study's authors purchased $128 worth of junk from a thrift store and sold the items for over $3,600 on Ebay after crafting a unique backstory about each object.

This experiment supports the value people place on a compelling narrative. But a good story also helps us remember facts. Studies show that humans can only remember 2 to 3 data points without a story, but can remember 8 or 9 once they fit them into the context of a story. Take a quick read of the two versions of the same advisor's summary and consider which you find to be more memorable.

**Summary 1:**
*First, as a registered representative of LPL Financial, and now, as an Investment Advisor Representative of LPL Financial, I provide professional investment advisory services to more than 100 individual clients who have more than $70,000,000 invested with me in securities through LPL Financial.*

**Summary 2:**
*I am an independent financial advisor supported by LPL Financial in San Diego, California. I have lived in San Diego all of my life, growing up in a small house in Lemon Grove, with two brothers and working class parents. My father served in the Navy for 40 years and my mother worked as a caterer and a baker while she raised me and my two younger brothers. Like many families in the 1940's and 1950's, we experienced some difficult times and struggled to make ends meet.*

*I realized from a young age the sense of peace, security and dignity that successful financial planning and investing can provide. This inspired me to enter the financial services industry fresh out of college, to help people just like my parents. Today, 36 years later, I remain committed to educating and inspiring my clients to take control of their finances. I enjoy building close, long-lasting relationships with my clients, many of which span decades and generations.*

*Over the years I have noticed that clients frequently call me to share their happy news, whether it's a new job or the birth of a child. I am also honored to serve as a shoulder to lean on during difficult times in life, such as a layoff, divorce, or death. It's my privilege to help clients on their journey of life and to celebrate their successes with them.*

One very successful financial advisor with HighTower Advisors engages prospects with the story of why planning is important to him. Before he was an advisor, he worked as the curator of his local art museum in a small town in the South. One summer, about 20 members of the museum set off for a trip overseas to tour the great museums of Europe.

Just after takeoff, their small plane crashed, killing several married couples with small children that had no life insurance in place. He witnessed the devastating effects in his community and was inspired to make a career change in order to offer comprehensive financial planning to the families in his community.

## Start With Why

These types of narratives allow prospects to understand why you do what you do and to put their faith in your services. Why did you get into this business and why do you come back each day? What drives you to serve your clients? Weave a story that illustrates your passion. The concept is highlighted in Simon Sinek's book, *Start with Why*. The book outlines how understanding why we do what we do helps clients and prospects trust us.

Here are some questions to help you get started writing:

- Why did you get into this business?
- Why did you become an *independent* advisor?
- What's the single most important thing you provide to clients?
- Why do your clients choose to work with you instead of someone else?
- What's the most difficult part of your job?

- Why is the most fulfilling part about your job?

- Describe a time you knew you had made a difference.

- What do you most hope to offer your clients?

Below are a few examples of "Start with Why" stories from advisors:

### Ricky Biel of BHA Wealth in Pasadena, California

*I started my practice as a financial advisor in February of 2000, at just 20 years old. While I was young, I was also ambitious and driven to help people become financially independent. This fire was lit back when I was just 12 years old. That year marked a Christmas to remember; in fact, it was one that I will never forget.*

*That Christmas, I didn't receive any gifts. None. Zero. Zilch. Nada. You get the point. My family was not in a financial position give any gifts that year. Although I understood, I shared the pain with my family and wanted to do something to change our lives. On that Christmas Day, I made a decision that I was going to be the one to lead my family to financial independence.*

*The pain of that day created an intense motivation that drove me to learn what it takes to create financial freedom. I decided that I would no longer be dependent on anyone to provide me with the things I wanted. That year, I started my own gardening business around my neighborhood. Ever since, I have always held a job and worked hard so that I could save, help my family, and enjoy what life has to offer. Instead of going to college after high school, I became a financial advisor to help people pursue financial freedom.*

### Deb Sims of Rancho Santa Fe, California

*As a wealth advisor to women for several decades, I have witnessed many women experience monumental financial and emotional tragedies due to unanticipated financial needs. I have also personally experienced some of the common fears shared between many of my clients. One of these events completely changed my life.*

*In 2005, I unexpectedly became a foster mother to four teenage girls, raising them alongside my three teenage daughters. Being a foster mother was no simple task and taking care of seven girls on my own while also running my practice as an independent wealth advisor added to my already overfilled plate. After nine months, my journey as a foster mother came to an end and the girls returned to their family. Each of our lives fell back into place and, over this past decade, I have watched these girls transform into strong and capable women.*

*I share this story because this experience changed my life, my perspective, and my purpose as a wealth advisor. While this was an overwhelming and sometimes frightening time in my life, by taking these risks I found a purpose for the rest of my life: helping women plan for the unexpected and take control of their financial lives so they can be prepared for any hardship that comes their way. Through workshops, events, and one-on-one planning, I challenge women to reach deep inside take control of their financial future.*

## Richard Ford in Lansing, Michigan

*I became a financial advisor because I want to help people. The most important thing I do for my clients is to truly listen to them in order to understand their story and what they're going through. My background is in counseling, with experience in crisis intervention counseling, senior end of life counseling, and suicide hotline counseling. I deeply care about my clients and I take my responsibility to them and their families very seriously.*

*In my career, I have seen many good hard working people end up without enough money to retire. I'm worried about our economy, our government, and our financial system. It's my goal to help the people I work with to protect their assets and make the most of their wealth.*

*As a member of the financial services industry, I am often frustrated with Wall Street. Large parts of the financial system have been set up to benefit at the expense of ordinary people trying to save for retirement. While large financial institutions have tremendous power, there are also many independent financial planning firms available to offer unbiased advice. I created an independent financial planning firm so that I can look out for my client's best interests, without allegiance to any insurance or investment company.*

*I believe that any middle class American nearing retirement should be concerned about the following statistics:*

- *The United States is $18 trillion in debt*

- *We have $122 trillion dollars in unfunded government liabilities*

- *Over 10,000 people per day turn 65 and sign up for Social Security and Medicare*

- *Social Security is facing a $134 trillion shortfall over the next 75 years*

*Why should you care about these figures? Most of us have been taught to put our retirement savings in tax-deferred accounts like 401(k) plans, 403(b) plans, and IRAs. But by putting money into these accounts, we delay paying taxes into the future. Unfortunately, when our government has to start paying for the debt it has accumulated, it will be forced to raise taxes in the future. Many people preparing to retire expect to withdraw a certain percentage from their tax-deferred accounts each month to pay their bills. If the government raises taxes from 25% to 45%, millions of retirees are not going to have as much income as they planned to have.*

*While the future of the economy may be troubling to investors, there are a variety of options to protect retirement funds against increasing tax rates. I help my clients invest after-tax dollars that will grow and be distributed tax-free. By investing after-tax dollars, retirees can decrease the uncertainty of their retirement income. If they don't spend their after-tax retirement savings, they may pass it to their heirs tax-free. To learn more, contact me today.*

For some, sharing your story is fun and the words will flow onto the page. For others, determining how to tell your story or what exactly to include can cause frustration and uncertainty. You'll likely ask yourself, "Am I oversharing? How much is too much? Will anyone really care?" If you are having trouble writing your "Why," have faith that people want to know what drives you and if you are still unsure of your story, share with a few clients for feedback.

## Step 4: End With Hobbies and Interests

After understanding why you do what you do, people want to know who you are. How do you spend your free time? What are your hobbies? What are your favorite sports teams? Do you *even* golf?! Which charitable causes are you passionate about? Do you have children or a dog? It can be simple, lighthearted, and fun. Here's how I end my LinkedIn summary:

*Claire lives in San Diego with her toxicologist husband (Josh), their dog (Wally), and their two American Paint Horses (Harley and Brandy). She has climbed Mt. Whitney three times and won a blue ribbon at the Del Mar Fair for her "Happy Hiker" trail mix.*

Sharing personal information allows prospects to find commonalities and get to know you, which is where a foundation of trust begins. List organizations you belong to and groups you're involved with to give an added SEO boost. Don't be shy in offering up personal details. I see over and over from advisors that once they make their profiles more personal, they start getting more messages and activity.

## Give People Something to Talk to You About

Keep in mind when writing this section that, in general, people are searching for commonalities with one another. This paragraph should allow them to find something they have in common with you, whether it be sports, family, or hobbies. This way, when they finally meet you in person, you'll have an icebreaker to talk about.

Through my own LinkedIn profile, I have benefited from my hobbies and interests section in building connections and relationships. Just last month, I received a message from one of the country's top advisors asking for help with his marketing. His message didn't start with business but with a question about mountain climbing in California, since I have climbed the highest peak in the state. If I hadn't listed my hobbies in my profile, I'm not sure we would have connected or had so much to talk about.

## Step 5: If You Get Stuck, Try Writing Backwards

Having trouble getting started? Try writing your bio backwards. Start with the personal side, including your hobbies and interests, then move on to your experience. Write the more technical opening paragraph last, when you're warmed up.

## Step 6: Add Your Specialties

I like to use 400-500 characters to dump in keywords that prospects might search for. At the very bottom of your summary where it won't be distracting, add a paragraph for "Specialties" and list all of the keywords for the services you offer. You can also add in specific locations and neighborhoods in this section.

*Specialties Include: Retirement Plan Design, Retirement Plan Administration, 401(k) Plans, Prevailing Wage Plans, ESOP, Cash Balance Plans, Defined Benefit Plans, Defined Contribution Plans, Pension Plans, Profit Sharing Plans. Serving clients in Phoenix, Scottsdale, and Yuma, Arizona.*

# Keep it Organized

Subheadings and bullet points are your best friend when keeping your profile orderly and organized. Remember that the summary section has a 2,000 character limit, but empty space surrounding bullet points and indentations do not count towards the limit. Using these conventions lets you spread out your summary and make it easier to read.

I recommend using a combination of subheading and bullet points to help people digest all that is featured in your profile and find what interests them quickly. The configuration will be unique to your profile, but here's one example:

### Summary
*Kevin Kersten is an Investment Advisor Representative with LPL Financial and a financial consultant with Kersten Wealth Management Group, a family run financial services firm located in Perrysburg, Ohio.*

### His Story
*Kevin grew up watching his father work in the financial services industry, helping people plan for the unexpected and prepare for retirement. He saw firsthand the positive impact his father had in their community and developed an interest in investments and financial markets. After graduating from The Ohio State University, he joined his older brother and father working in the family firm.*

### Meet Kevin
*Kevin resides in Perrysburg, Ohio with his wife and three children. He enjoys coaching children's soccer teams, attending their swim meets and other sporting events, as well as golfing with his family.*

*Kevin and his family attend the First United Methodist Church in Perrysburg. In the fall, they enjoy watching football as a family, supporting the*

Buckeyes. When he's not working, Kevin spends his time exercising and working on his golf game.

### Fun Facts

- *Radio Show: Money Sense, Saturdays, 7 AM on News Talk 1370, WSPD*

- *Head Coach: His daughters' soccer teams*

- *Sports Team: Buckeyes*

- *Hobby: Golfing*

### Specialties

*Financial Planning Specialties Include: Investment Management, Retirement Planning, IRA Distribution Planning, IRA Rollovers, 401(k) Rollovers, Intergenerational Wealth Transfer, Insurance Analysis, Company Stock Option Analysis. Securities and Advisory services offered through LPL Financial, a Registered Investment Advisor. Member FINRA/SIPC. For hyperlinks to FINRA and SIPC, please refer to 'Contact Info' section above.*

# Polish and Publish

It's helpful to disregard grammar and wording when you're writing the first draft of your profile. Getting your thoughts and logic down is the hardest part. Wordsmithing those thoughts is easier once they're on paper. Once you've followed these six steps, proofread and fine tune your bio.

Ask a friend or assistant to give it a quick review to make sure there are no spelling or grammatical errors. My favorite free online grammar editor is Grammarly.com and will clue you in to any errors. Once you're happy with the result, send it to compliance, feature it on your LinkedIn profile, and consider updating your website bio, too.

# Consider a LinkedIn Company Page

If there's another advisor in your firm, you may want to create a LinkedIn Company page. Company pages promote your firm and act like a profile for your brand. They can link to profiles of company employees and LinkedIn users can "follow" company updates. You post to company pages in the same way you would share content in your own updates.

I recommend company pages for large groups, but not for smaller firms or single advisors, as they are better off investing that time and energy posting to their own profile. People generally want to do business more with a person than a brand, so single advisors promoting their profile and company page can dilute their efforts.

One note about company pages, LinkedIn requires an email address with a unique domain for each company page, so if your work email address is @lpl.com, you will not be able to create a company page, you would need an email address ending in @yourcompany.com that has not previously been used to set up a page.

If you've completed the process in this chapter, your profile is now better than 90% of advisors' profiles out there. Congratulations! What's next? In the next chapter, we'll cover some advanced tips and tricks to build out your profile and make you look like a true LinkedIn professional.

CHAPTER 3

# Supercharging Your Profile

I f your LinkedIn profile was a car, the last chapter built the engine and got it running. This chapter will add paint, wheels, and sound system to make you stand out as a LinkedIn power user.

A standalone profile is great for illustrating who you are and supporting credibility, but a supercharged profile acts like your own LinkedIn interactive website, where people can learn exactly what you do, see samples of your work, watch videos, click through your presentations, read your publications, and get to know you better.

The goals of building out your profile are similar to the goals of an effective website:

- Keep people on your profile longer

- Get them to interact with your content

- Invite them to take the next step

To accomplish these goals, we'll use all of the available LinkedIn features and tricks.

## Fill Out Every Section

When you're building your LinkedIn profile, the system automatically gives you a "Profile Strength Score" of completeness as a percentage. It's easy to reach 70%, but it's exponentially harder to get to 100%. The only way to achieve a perfect score of "All Star" is to fill out all of the LinkedIn sections. Having a higher score means that LinkedIn will list you higher in search results.

Here are the sections we'll need to fill out:

- Experience
- Education
- Courses
- Certifications
- Organizations
- Volunteer
- Languages
- Publications
- Interests
- Following

## Experience

The experience section is critical for job seekers and recruiters, but for most advisors, it won't serve as much more than a walk down memory lane. At best, you can use this section to build credibility if you worked for a large financial institution before you started your own firm. If your only experience before your financial services career was manual labor in a cannery (true for my Dad), this section can be tricky to optimize.

Ideally, your experience section will include three to five relevant positions, demonstrating a promotion in job title and responsibility between each role. If you list too many positions, you look like a flight risk. Too few compromises your perceived experience level.

Think through your professional positions and choose the three to five that are most relevant to your current role and that you're most proud of. To list each position on your profile, you'll click "Add Position" and then enter your job title and the company name.

## Link to the LinkedIn Company Page

LinkedIn Company Pages are like profiles, but for companies. There is a search feature to find profiles based on past employer, so if the company exists on LinkedIn as a company page, be sure to link to it so that people can search for you by company. This will also display the company's logo in that section of your profile, which adds visual interest.

Next, list the dates of employment and try not to overlap two jobs unless they actually were held concurrently, in which case it is best practice to list "Held Concurrently to X, Y, and Z position" in the description.

For each position, you'll want to add a description of your role at that company. The subject of writing resumes is a topic for a whole different book, but the most common mistake folks make when writing their resume is they list *their duties*, not *their accomplishments*.

In the "Description" section for each position, list your most extraordinary accomplishments in that role and *how you helped your clients and the company succeed*. Wherever possible, use concrete, quantifiable metrics. Here are two examples:

**Do Not List Duties:**
*Marketed 401(k) plans to Financial Advisors in the Georgia, Florida, Alabama territory.*

**Do List Concrete Achievements:**
*Grew AUM by $1 million in first four months, retained 98% of client accounts annually, and scored 96% on client satisfaction survey.*

Three to five bullet points for each position is sufficient to show your competency and record of success. Don't get hung up or spend too much time on these, as they do not get much exposure unless you are a job seeker.

## Hide Disclosures Under Experience If Possible

Have you ever dreamt, just for a minute or two, that you were able to market your firm without compliance? I share this dream. The closest feeling you may ever get to this is publishing your LinkedIn Summary without disclosures.

Some major broker-dealers allow advisors to put disclosures in the "Experience" section of their profile, instead of under "Summary." This allows you to use all of the 2,000 characters in the summary section to showcase yourself and hide your disclosures under your current position. The experience section is not critical for keyword searches and does not get many readers, so it's nice if you are able to list your required disclosures here.

## Education

The Education section of your profile is important, as studies show that awareness of an advisor's education helps prospects trust their expertise. Additionally, listing your schools allows fellow alumni to find you by a "School" keyword search, which we'll review in detail later. Your education section can also give you access to private alumni groups.

It's best practice to add your college degree and graduate degree, if applicable. If you have a college degree, you will not usually list your high school education. If you do not have a college or graduate degree, you will want to list your high school education and give special care towards the other parts of your profile, such as volunteer and organizations, to increase your perceived experience.

To add your education, navigate to the education section and click "Add Education." The process is similar to adding a job, you'll find the school by a search and link to the LinkedIn page for that school, which is similar to a company page. Then you'll enter the dates, degree, and field of study.

Next, list all "Activities and Societies" in wich you were involved, including clubs, sports teams, fraternal organizations, debate teams, volunteer causes, and so on. Remember how much pressure there was to be involved in different organizations in college? This is where you finally get credit for all those activities.

Finally, similar to the description you listed under each job above, you'll list a few bullet point achievements from your time at each school. These could range anywhere from clubs you started, to athletic awards, to success in coursework. Think of at least three things you accomplished during your time at school and feature them here.

Here are my accomplishments from business school:

- *Successful business case analysis of web-based technology transfer marketplace in partnership with UC San Diego and the U.S. Department of Defense*

- *New Product Development with Hewlett Packard Inkjet Consumer Systems Group*

- *Business Development and Distribution Strategy for Foundation for Women Microloan Coffee Network*

## Courses

If you remember any of the courses you took back in college and they're relevant to your current role, go ahead and list them under the "Courses" section, which is not within the Education section, but under its own heading. You'll list the name of the course and then select at which school you took the course.

Because I took the course *Modern Portfolio Theory* from Dr. Harry Markowitz himself, I list the course on my profile. My very favorite course from college was *Taxation and Behavior*, a subject I'm still fascinated with, so I list that course as well in case anyone from my network wants to have a heated discussion about the possibility of a flat income tax.

## Certifications

Research by behavioral economist Dr. Daniel Crosby has shown that prospects' behavior in choosing an advisor is influenced by both education and credentials. However, an interesting insight from the research is that prospects don't typically understand or care which credentials you hold, only that you have some letters behind your name.

For this reason, I wouldn't start studying for the CFP in order to fill up your LinkedIn profile, but if you do have your CFP, AIF, CFA, CPA, CFC,

CLU or any other alphabet soup, include them under "Certifications." If you do not have any of those designations, list your securities licenses in this section, whether you hold Series 6, 7, 66, 65, Life and Health licenses, etc. You'll enter the name of the certification, the authority (for example, FINRA), and the dates held.

## Organizations

The organization section is where you get credit for all of your extracurricular activities. This is a great place to illustrate if you are involved in your community and also give people something to find in common with you. Don't list volunteer organization here, since they will appear in their own section. This section is for community, civic, and business groups.

Here, you'll want to list every organization that you are involved with, from advisory boards, to Rotary Club, to Toastmasters, to Youth Soccer coaching. For each specific group, click "Add Organization" and list the name, the position you held, the date, and any additional notes, such as achievements or honors.

## What About Religion and Politics?

The organization section of you profile is where you would list church affiliation if you participate in a leadership function or any political group affiliations. I understand why advisors are hesitant to list political organizations if they know a significant portion of their current clients do not share the same political views.

However, I encourage advisors to list church affiliations and other groups because I believe affiliation is more powerful in attracting like-minded prospects (who you'll enjoy working with) than turning off those who don't share your views. In the end, it's a personal choice that must be made based on your comfort with sharing your beliefs and who you would like to work with in the future.

# Volunteer

LinkedIn likes volunteering. They've adapted their platform to highlight volunteer endeavors and help users find others interested in volunteering towards their causes. They also have a section where you can donate your expertise pro-bono.

Go ahead and add every organization you volunteer with, even if you are not currently active. Click on "Add Volunteer Experience" and list the organization name to link to their company page. Then, enter your role, which category of cause the group belongs to, a date range (helpful for past endeavors) and a description of any achievements, such as *Raised $50,000 for annual gala.*"

In the volunteer section, you'll also want to fill out any volunteer opportunities you are looking for, how you may like to donate your time and talent, causes you care about, and organizations you support (donate to). These are all searchable by keyword through the advanced search function.

# Languages

This part is easy! List English, followed by any other languages and your proficiency level for each.

# Publications

This is where you list any books or other publications you've authored. Add the title, publisher, date, website if applicable, and a description. Even if you've authored an eBook or Whitepaper, go ahead and list it here.

# Interests

The "Interests" section is within "Additional Info" and is important because each interest you list here is searchable as a keyword. Within "Additional Info," list all hobbies and interests separated by a comma, as well as your birthday.

The last section is "Advice for Contacting Me," where I recommend listing some version of:

*Tom only takes on new clients he believes he can help and enjoys meeting new people to understand their unique goals and challenges. To get a second opinion on your financial plan or to meet to discuss how the XYZ Capital Management team may be able to help your family, call our office at (888) 778-1900.*

## Following

The last section of your profile isn't actually a profile section, though we'll treat it so because it appears at the bottom of your profile. The "Following" section displays all the key influencers on LinkedIn you are following, in the order of how many followers *they* have. This section gives a glimpse of who you respect in your industry and which experts you get your news from.

Go ahead and list your investment and business heros here by searching for their profile in the search bar, visiting their profile, and clicking the blue button to "Follow" them. This will display their name and photo on your profile and add their updates to your activity feed. This section also shows the companies, schools, and news sources that you follow, so you may want to review and adjust as you see fit.

## Take it to the Next Level

You've now added all of the sections required to be a LinkedIn superstar. You may also want to add other sections such as patents, awards, honors, test scores, etc. if they apply to you. Here are a few extra steps to take your profile to the next level.

### Get a Custom URL

The litmus test for whether someone is an amateur LinkedIn user is whether they have a "Custom URL," which means that instead of your LinkedIn profile link being: *www.linkedin.com/in/ronhechtsb145243757*, it will read *www.linkedin.com/in/yourname.*

A custom URL is free and takes less than 30 second to create. Go to "Edit Profile," then click the little tiny gear symbol next to your existing URL, which is under your photo.

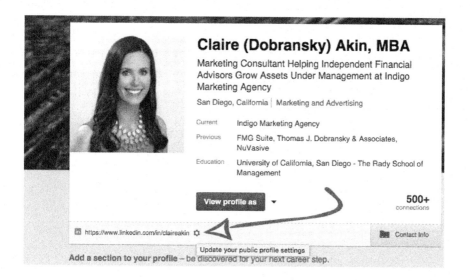

You will be redirected to the "Edit My Public Profile Screen." From here, you'll want to click the small pencil button next to "Your Public Profile URL" to edit your URL. This will allow you to create a vanity URL with your name, as long as no one has already taken it. If you have a common name, you may need to put your last name first or add your middle name.

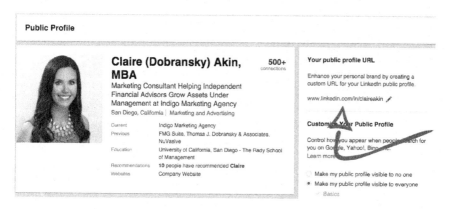

Once you have a custom URL, list it on your website, marketing collateral, and email signature to invite folks to connect with you.

Your profile is shaping up but we're not done yet. Now it's time to supercharge each main section of your profile by adding content to them.

## Add Multimedia Content

The ability to add multimedia content to your profile is relatively new, but growing quickly. Profiles with multimedia content are given preferential treatment and can actually help with the SEO of your website if you link back to content you have hosted there.

The types of content I recommend adding to your static profile are:

- Videos

- Slideshows

- Documents

- Websites

- Brochures

- Infographics

You can add content in two ways — by linking to a website where your content resides or by uploading a file. If you link to a website, LinkedIn will create a thumbnail that visitors can click on to go to that site. Below are the types of files supported that you may upload directly.

*Presentations*

- *.pdf*

- *.ppt*

- *.pps*

- *.pptx*

- *.ppsx*

- *.pot*

- *.potx*

- *.odp*

*Documents*

- *.pdf*
- *.doc*
- *.docx*
- *.rtf*
- *.odt*

*Images*

- *.png*
- *.gif*
- *.jpg*
- *.jpeg*

I've seen advisors take advantage of multimedia content by uploading presentations, whitepapers, brochures, marketing collateral, infographics, team photos, and more. Any item that will help people get to know your firm is helpful. If you have other interests, such as a non-business related blog, you can list it here for some color.

## I recommend adding the following to your summary:

- Your business website
- Any business-related videos
- Any compliance-approved presentations that explain what you do

Then, add one or two other multimedia items to each job within your "Experience" sections if you can. More than anything, these items add variety and interest to a profile that is otherwise text-based.

## Reorder Your Profile

Most advanced LinkedIn users do not know that you can choose the order in which your main profile sections appear. This strategy will allow you to have a truly custom profile. If you're an author, you likely want to put "Publications" first. If you are seeking a job, you'll want to put experience and skills first. The order depends on your unique profile, but it's worth considering which parts of your profile are strongest and listing them in that order.

All else being equal, I recommend the following order for an average advisor who has been at their own firm for over 10 years (and so experience is less important):

1. Summary

2. Education

3. Certifications

4. Experience

5. Volunteer

6. Publications

However, if you are a prolific volunteer, or you have impressive publications, you'll want to reorder those sections accordingly.

## Your Profile Photo

As we reviewed before, profiles with photos get 13 times the views as profiles without photos. I recommend using the same photo that you have on your website for cohesion. The photo should be a professional headshot in business attire.

If you don't have a headshot, it is easy and inexpensive to get one. Go to Yelp.com and type in "Headshot" or "Photographer." Find a photographer that has 4 or more stars in your area and contact them. Often, professional photographers have regular business headshot days in their studios for $50-$100. If for some reason, you are resistant to getting a headshot, take a normal photo and turn it black and white using Photoshop.com's express photo editor. Black and white photos look more professional that a casual shot in color.

If your profile photo is more than 3-5 years old, it's time for an update. Try to get a photo that looks like you, or at least the best version of yourself. If you wear glasses, wear them in your photo so people recognize you. Crop the photo from just below the shoulders to no higher than just above your head.

## Your Background photo

Facebook pioneered the idea of a background photo, which is an image behind your profile photo that spans across the page. Twitter added them next, followed by LinkedIn. Adding a background photo is important to polish your profile, because if you do not add one, the background will show up as a default blue blur.

I recommend that your Twitter, Facebook, and LinkedIn profile background images are all the same high-quality photo that also appears on your website. This helps present a cohesive brand across platforms and allows people to recognize your brand.

Great background photos include images such as the skyline of your city, a recognizable local landmark, or a visual that represents your brand. If you have a photo of yourself working with clients, giving a presentation, or a book you'd like to promote, those can make nice backgrounds as well.

The challenge is that a background image size is 1425 by 400 pixels, which is incredibly long and skinny. The only portion that shows up behind your profile are the edges, which rules out most photos, where the object is in the center. They are also very large, so all but the highest resolution photos will look distorted. You can see the areas that will be visible below.

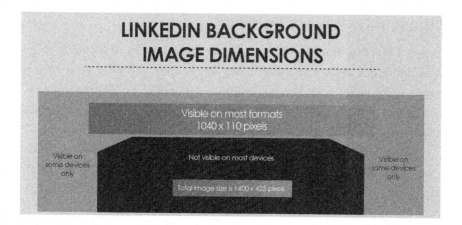

If you're having a hard time finding an image that will work, Google *"linkedin background images 1400 x 425"* and select from one of the many photos of nature, technology, textures, etc. You should be able to find an image that is relevant to your brand or personality. As long as you have a background photo, your profile passes this test.

Here are a few good examples of background photos that add to the context of a profile:

## Adjust Your Privacy Settings

This is LinkedIn, not the Witness Protection Program. The goal is to get your name out there and make it easy for people who need your help to locate and contact you. For this reason, I recommend adjusting your privacy settings so that the public can see your profile, photo, and contact information.

To do this, click on the same little gear next to your profile URL, under your photo that we used to change your Custom URL. Then, on the right hand side, under "Customize Your Public Profile," click on "Make My Public Profile Visible to Everyone" and check all the boxes.

◉ Make my public profile visible to everyone

☑ Basics

☑ Picture

☑ Headline

☑ Websites

☑ Posts

☑ Summary

☑ Current Positions

   ☑ Details

☑ Past Positions

   ☑ Details

☑ Education

   ☑ Details

☑ Certifications

☑ Publications

☑ Languages

☑ Volunteer Experiences & Causes

☑ Courses

☑ Skills

☑ Interests

☑ Organizations

☑ Recommendations

☑ Groups

**Save**   Cancel

# Grow Your Network

Now that your profile is 100% complete and looks perfect, you'll want to expand your reach. For every effort you are going to invest in LinkedIn, you can double the payoff by doubling your network. It increases your ROI on your LinkedIn time and grows your referral base. There are two avenues to growing your network, adding connections, and joining groups.

## Upload Contacts

The easiest and most effective way to add connections is by uploading your contacts' email addresses. LinkedIn can search all of its users by email address and automatically connect you with users in your email address book. There are two ways to add your email contacts, by linking through your email via the LinkedIn interface built for this, or by uploading a spreadsheet of email addresses.

In either case, you will start by going to Connections, then "Add Connections." You can either connect an existing email account including Gmail, Hotmail, Yahoo, etc. However, for most advisors, this is not helpful because they are typically required to use compliance archived email servers. In these cases, you'll need to import your contacts.

To do this, the trick is to export your contacts from your customer relationship management (CRM) system or email server as an excel spreadsheet or .CSV file. The process to do this is different for each email server or CRM, but it is typically a built in functionality that isn't too difficult. If you do a quick Google search for the system you are using, you will find step-by-step directions. For Outlook 2010, here are the steps:

1. Open Outlook 2010 and click File > Options.

2. When the Outlook Options window opens, click Advanced.

3. In the Import and Export Wizard window, select the Export to a file option, then Next.

4. In the File Type option, select Comma Separated Values (Windows) option to create a CSV file.

If you have trouble, call tech support and they can walk you through the process. If you can't export as a .CSV file, that's no problem, just export as an Excel file, then open the spreadsheet in Excel. Click on File, then Export, and select ".CSV" to change the file type. Once you save the .CSV version of your spreadsheet, you can upload directly to LinkedIn by clicking on "Import File" in the "Add Connections" section.

Remember to import email addresses from your various systems, whether you have a CRM, email address book, financial planning software, email newsletter list, etc. By uploading as many of your contacts as you can, you maximize your network.

**One Caution:**

*When you upload a spreadsheet to LinkedIn, it gives you a prompt that explains how many of your contacts are currently on LinkedIn and ask if you would like to connect. Select yes. Then, watch out! It will give you another prompt that looks almost identical to the first prompt, but this time with a list of your connections who are not on LinkedIn and asks if you'd like to invite them. Say no! This is a way for LinkedIn to get more users, but the automatic emails the system sends on your behalf can be confusing and annoying to folks in your network who are not on LinkedIn. If you've gotten these emails from people inviting you to join LinkedIn, this is likely what happened.*

## Join Groups

The second way to expand your influence and improve your ROI for LinkedIn is by joining groups. There are two types of groups: open and closed. The group administrator decides whether the group will be open or closed. Open groups add members who request to join automatically and closed groups require administrator approval of membership requests. I recommend joining both types of groups. Closed groups can be more exclusive with less noise and promotions, but may take a few days for the administrator to log in and approve your request.

To search for groups to join, go to "Interests," then "Groups." Then, you'll be at a page that gives you a newsfeed of your group activity. From here, click on "Discover" to find new groups to join.

The "Discover" feature is powerful because LinkedIn will suggest groups for you to join based on your network. This saves you the time and energy of searching for groups where you and your clients' interests overlap. Go ahead and join any of the groups suggested that you find relevant. There is a maximum of 52 groups per person, but you will be hard-pressed to find that many groups you find uniquely relevant.

The next way to find groups to join is to search in the main search bar for your city, neighborhood, or locality. Then, in the search results, click on the filter on the far left to display only "Groups." Request to join local groups to increase your exposure within your geographic location.

Finally, a great way to join groups where your prospects may be is to look at the profiles of your top clients and join the groups they belong to. These could vary from employer groups, industry groups, charitable groups, groups with similar interests, etc.

Other effective groups to join include:

- Business Networking Groups (CPAs, Lawyers, etc.)
- Alumni Groups (College and High School)
- Groups of Your Organizations (Toastmasters International)
- Industry Groups (Engineers in Michigan)
- Special Interest Groups (Classic Car Aficionados of Grass Valley, CA)

## Update Regularly

Now that your profile is extraordinary and your network is strong, you'll want to update both regularly. I recommend updating your profile at least every six months and uploading your email address book at the same frequency.

Anytime you get a piece of marketing collateral approved by compliance for public release, add it to your profile. This increases the depth of your profile and keeps it up to date, which improves SEO. By using LinkedIn on a regular basis, you'll come across awesome profiles that you want to emulate. Challenge yourself to keep making your profile better and better over time.

You officially have a standout LinkedIn profile that's 100% complete.

Congrats! Only 50.5% of all LinkedIn users have completed 100% of their profile, and users who do so are 40 times more likely to receive opportunities through LinkedIn. Next, you'll want to buckle up as I reveal the tried and true process for generating high-value referrals using LinkedIn.

# CHAPTER 4

# How to Use LinkedIn to Generate Referrals

The logic behind asking for introductions is nothing new; many of you have probably been employing some version of this strategy for decades. But today we can use LinkedIn as a tool to easily identify who we want to be introduced to, then find a mutual connection who already knows and trusts us to make the introduction. Another advantage is that you can easily qualify prospects on LinkedIn by their job title, seniority level, or experience to save time and focus your efforts on well-qualified prospects.

While using LinkedIn strategically to support your referral process is powerful, it takes some time to build a proper foundation. Just as you wouldn't ask a new acquaintance for referrals without building trust with them first, you'll want to take some time to establish your online relationship with your network and prime the pump for introductions. Let's walk through how you can set yourself up for long-term online networking success.

## The Giver, the Taker, and the Matcher

On LinkedIn, and in life, there are generally three types of people: the giver, the taker, and the matcher. We all can identify characters from our lives that fall into each category. The takers leave us feeling exhausted, put out, or taken advantage of after interactions. Givers, on the other hand, are those kind folks that look out for others and remember your birthday even though you forgot theirs last year.

Most of us are matchers, decent and considerate people who automatically feel compelled to reciprocate when someone does something nice for us. About half the time, we do something nice for others for no reason. However, our social norms feel violated if we do too many nice things without any reciprocation. That is because there happens to be a strong social rule called reciprocity.

## The Reciprocity Principle

Reciprocity is a social phenomenon that makes us feel obligated to return the favor after someone does something for us. The principle is behind a bevy of marketing and sales strategies, including those charity mailings that provide you with a gift that makes you feel bad if you don't donate in return. The same motivation delivers a mint from the waiter with your restaurant bill; research shows that dining tips increase 20% with a thoughtfully placed treat.

The idea works in a negative way, too. The "eye for an eye" principle is coded into our legal and justice systems. Freeloaders and moochers are seen as a drain on societies and most cultures look down upon those who take without contributing. Anthropologists claim that reciprocity is a uniquely human trait and that we adapted into civilizations only because we were able to reliably to share goods.

It's important to note that reciprocity works even when we don't like the person employing the technique. Researchers showed in one study that when a stranger asks us for a favor, our response depends on how likeable we rate the stranger. However, if that stranger first brings us a candy or a drink, the principle of reciprocity overrides how much we like the person. We tend to comply with their request even if we dislike them.

# Who is a Giver?

There are effective (and manipulative) ways to use reciprocity in negotiations and persuasion. However, in our LinkedIn referral process, we'll focus on using this power for good to help folks in our network. Most of the advisors I work with are givers by nature, and not just to get something in return. They typically like to help people and enjoy networking as well as making introductions.

In my presentations, I often ask the audience how many people in the room have ever set someone up on a blind date. There is usually a strong show of hands. I am proud to have two marriages as a result of the blind dates I've set up. But there are also a few close friends who dated, then things didn't work out, and now I can't invite them both to the same party. Why would anyone decide to go out of their way to introduce to people they know, fully aware that the situation could end in social division and awkwardness? It's simple. Many of us are connectors at heart and like making introductions.

You probably have clients or referral partners who are givers. Anyone who has ever sent you a referral in the past is likely to do it again. People who make introductions and share information with you are likely givers. Make note of those in your network who display the characteristics of a giver and make sure you're repaying the favors.

You also may want to take a little care to make sure you're not acting like a taker. A friend of mine from business school started a company that recently sold for $350 million. He mentioned that since the news of his success broke, he can open up his Facebook and LinkedIn profiles and see the dozens of messages from folks he hasn't heard from in years asking him for something. Before you ask someone for a favor, make sure you've done something nice for them in the past six months.

# Meet the World's Best Networker

Forbes has ranked Michael Port as the "World's Best Networker," even above Keith Ferrazzi, author of the networking bible Never Eat Alone. Michael has thousands of followers, is a New York Times bestselling author, and prolific professional speaker.

Obviously well-connected, he also happens to be a nice guy and a natural giver. A few months ago I reached out to him to ask him if he would read and endorse my client's new book. He got back to me within a day and endorsed the book within a week. I was impressed! Because of my human need for reciprocity, I am automatically on the lookout for ways to repay him.

I've used his step-by-step system to grow my network and connect with the top influencers in our industry. He coaches entrepreneurs and leaders to systematically grow their influence each day by doing three things:

1. **Introduce two people who don't know each other, but should.** For example, if you're a terrible golfer but you know two guys who are excellent golfers with business interests in common, make the introduction.

2. **Send a piece of relevant information to two people in your network.** This could be anything from an interesting article about the Chicago Bears for your client who is a long-time fan to a trail recommendation for a friend who loves hiking.

3. **Share compassion.** Online and in real life, we all love validation, acknowledgment, and praise. Spend a minute each day to give an online "high five" to someone in your network.

Each day you adhere to this process, you'll touch five folks (two people you introduce, two messages you send, and one person you praise). Each work week, this adds up to 25 folks. Over the course of a month, you'll reconnect with 100 folks in your network. The process takes about 10 minutes to complete each day and is often enjoyable and interesting.

## How To Be a Giver

Many of the advisors I work with understand the benefits of being a giver and buy into the process I've outlined above. However, when they get back to their office and sit in front of their computers, questions come up. Let's review some examples so you understand exactly how to make it happen.

## Offering Introductions

This is probably the trickiest of the three to get right, but there are several ways to make introductions that add value for both parties involved. You can send an email to both contacts and say "Jim, meet Bob. Bob, meet Jim. You both are scratch golfers and I think you might enjoy meeting one another. There's an upcoming charity tournament I'll be participating in. Would you like to join me?"

Another option is to introduce folks whose business interests overlap, "Hi Mary, It was nice to get together with you last week. Our conversation about your software project made me think of Sue. Sue runs a software development company and may be able to point you in the right direction. I've copied her on this email." Introducing current clients to non-clients has the added benefit of creating an opportunity for your client to share their experience working with your firm.

A fail-proof option is to help the children or grandchildren of people in your network find jobs or learn more about a career that interests them. "Hi, John! Congratulations on your son's graduation with an engineering degree. I wanted to take a moment to introduce you to Doug. Doug is a senior level engineer with Boeing and would be happy to take a look at your son's resume and offer feedback."

Here's a real life introduction I made last month: "Hi Larry, I wanted to introduce you to Ken. Ken is a third party administrator in Phoenix. You both are involved with the Chandler Arizona Little League organization. He's a great resource for your 401(k) opportunities and I think you'd enjoy meeting him." It turns out they met for coffee, recognized each other from Little League games, and are planning to do business together in the future.

## Sending Information

This is the easiest of the three and you've likely been sharing information this way for years, but nevertheless, here are a few examples:

"Barry, I'm looking forward to seeing you next month. In the meantime, I came across this Phil Mickelson article I thought would give you some laughs."

"Hi Linda, Hope you are having a nice holiday season. My wife came across this great shop for all things equestrian that she really enjoyed. I thought I'd share their website with you. Merry Christmas to you and the horses!"

"Good Morning Roger, How's is your latest robotics project coming? A client of mine just released a new book, "Unmanned Systems of WWI and WWII" that I thought you'd find interesting. I've purchased a Kindle copy for you at the link below. Enjoy."

## Giving Praise

Do you remember the good old days when you'd pick up the phone and call someone to congratulate them on a new baby, new job, or new house? When was the last time you were on the receiving end of an old fashioned Happy Birthday phone call? Anthropologists assure me that these acts of communication happened as recently as the 1990s, though texting and emailing has replaced them today.

Everyone loves to get praise, especially with a real live phone call. Social media acts as a great trigger to pick up the phone and call. Log onto LinkedIn or Facebook and scroll through your news feed to look for new grandchildren, new jobs, or new retirements. When possible, call to congratulate. If you don't have a phone number, sending an email or LinkedIn message to say congratulations is also nice.

## Surprise and Delight Gifts

Once you've laid your foundation on social media by engaging with your network each week, it's time to crank it up a notch and take the first big step in the reciprocity equation. Research from The Oeschli Institute shows that 71% of top advisors give gifts to people in their network at least once per year.

A surprise and delight gift is a small, thoughtful, and unexpected gift. The more personal and less expensive, the better. You can't purchase a set of 100 of something and send them out. To make it personal, you'll need to think about each person's interests and passions.

If you're a good advisor, and I bet you are, you probably spend about half of your client meetings discussing non-financial topics including your clients' families, hobbies, and interests. Make a note of what's important to them so you can follow up each year with a thoughtful gift.

A great example of a surprise and delight give is the coffee table book. For example, one of my clients has a fascination with the Hubble Space Telescope, so I gave him a great coffee table book with images from Hubble.

An added bonus of your surprise and delight gift is when it resides in the recipient's home or is used for entertaining. This way, when your client is using the gift or a guest comments on it, you are top of mind:

"Great coffee table book!"

"Well thanks, my financial advisor got it for me."

"Wow, I really need some financial help. Is your advisor any good?"

Other examples of good surprise and delight gifts are unusual magazine subscriptions, such as "Birding Magazine" for your favorite birder. Tickets to athletic events are great, as long as they are under the $100 per year, per person in accordance with the FINRA limit. Books are great options too, especially if your contact is going through a difficult time. One advisor I work with keeps a variety of books to send to clients dealing with divorce, death, the loss of a parent, or post-retirement depression.

If you get stuck thinking of something personal, send a birthday gift. Everyone sends treats and gifts for the holidays, but birthdays and anniversaries are often overlooked. Birthdays are listed on investment accounts for clients and are often on Facebook in the "About" section for non-clients. If you have single, divorced, or widowed clients, send a treat on Valentine's Day to really stand out.

Clients who employ this strategy typically keep a spreadsheet of folks in their network who are good referral sources, including notes on individual interests. Then, they jot down ideas for specific gifts or have their administrative assistant choose one online.

# What To Do on LinkedIn Every Day

Being successful on LinkedIn is a lot like staying fit. To keep in shape, you have to put diet and exercise as a priority on a consistent basis. LinkedIn works best if you put a few minutes towards your efforts on a regular basis, not all at once. I recommend spending your first cup of coffee at the office on LinkedIn. Here's what to do:

1. **Connect with everyone you meet.** The first step of strengthening your online networking muscles is to always work toward expanding your network. Be sure to connect with all clients, not just your top clients, as well as everyone you meet while networking or socializing. The larger your network, the more opportunities you have to find qualified prospects. My rule of thumb for who to connect with is anyone who you have met in person, worked with virtually, or would feel comfortable introducing to someone else in your network.

2. **Reach out to referral partners.** Spend some time each week to reach out to CPAs, estate planning attorneys, lawyers, real estate agents, and other potential referral partners. Send a quick message introducing yourself and explaining who you work with and how you can help. Ask about their unique specialty to understand what they do best.

3. **Seek out centers of influence.** Centers of influence, or COIs, are the movers and shakers in your locality. The mayor, the top business leaders, the lady who works at the coffee cart and has her finger on the pulse of your town. Make sure these folks know exactly what you do so they can introduce you to others and share your information. One trick to helping them understand your firm is to invite them in for a "mock client meeting" so they get an introduction to your philosophy, your process, and your team.

4. **Share valuable content.** Content is at the core of our LinkedIn strategy, and we'll dig deep into that topic in the next chapter. But each day, you'll want to spend a minute or two sharing content that your network will find valuable.

5. **Respond to all messages.** The etiquette for responding to Facebook messages is about 24 hours, 48 hours for LinkedIn, and only two hours for Twitter messages. For this reason, I caution advisors from pursuing a Twitter-centric strategy unless they can commit to quick responses every day. To keep up-to-date and have good LinkedIn

manners, be sure to check and respond to your messages on at least Monday, Wednesday, and Friday.

6. **Engage with others.** Similar to offering praise, engaging with others is a nice way to show that you are interested in what they're doing. Read their articles, "like" their posts, and comment on their discussions. This also helps you understand what your clients and prospects are reading, sharing, and consuming online, which is helpful when we create your custom content strategy in the next chapter.

7. **Discuss within groups.** LinkedIn groups are powerful because they allow you to interact with people you don't know. Spend some time perusing the discussions within your groups, sharing content, and offering your two cents. I recently landed a big speaking engagement after an industry leader read a blog post I shared within one of our mutual groups. Don't limit your groups to business, and keep it fun by discussion your passions in groups of like-minded enthusiasts. One of my clients spends this time chatting in LinkedIn classic cat groups.

8. **Follow key influencers.** One of my advisors likes to say, "I've never had a new idea in my life, so if you steal from me, you're stealing twice." Following key influencers is an excellent opportunity to learn what top networkers are doing and copy what works. You can follow people without being connected to them by clicking the "Follow" button on the dropdown menu next to "Connect." You can also get exposure by liking and commenting on key influencers' content, because other folks in their network will see your activity.

9. **Browse the news.** Your LinkedIn newsfeed is a great place to read articles, see what people are sharing, and watch videos. It's not designed for breaking news, but there is a treasure trove of specific, insightful content that experts in your network publish directly to LinkedIn.

10. **Make introductions!** You can actually introduce two people in your network directly through LinkedIn by going to one contact's

profile and clicking on the drop down next to "Message" and selecting "Share." This automatically sends a message offering to introduce the recipient to contact you shared. This is great for helping someone in your network with a job search or introducing two business colleagues. The downside is that both folks have to be relatively proficient with LinkedIn, so I only use the feature when I'm sure they are pretty active on the site.

## Those Who Don't Buy Can Still Refer

The philosophy of marketing that I teach my clients focuses not on trying to sell, but on helping prospects find you when they need you most. To do this, we need to get crystal clear on who you serve and how you help them. If your network doesn't understand what makes you different and who your clients are, they can't refer business to you. I coach advisors to make their niche so clear that even those who don't buy can still refer.

By embracing a specialization and helping your network understand what you do, you empower them to offer a solution when they come across folks that could benefit from your advice. Your referral pipeline is strengthened when conversations go from "I think Tom is in finance" to "Tom helps divorcing spouses get a fair and equitable settlement" or "my neighbor helps baby boomers who own businesses catch up on their retirement savings in a hurry."

Consider what you would most like your connections to say about you and practice saying it until it comes naturally to you. Share it with folks you meet, your existing clients, and centers of influence. Weave this into your content strategy and LinkedIn profile. Over time, you'll become "The Guy/Gal" for whatever specific thing you do best.

## Identify Who You Want to Meet

You may be familiar with popular sales tactics in the past that included making a list of your top 10 dream clients and keeping your eyes open for opportunities to meet them. My dad works with the affluent in La Jolla, California and one of the top local prospects on his list was the late author Theodor Seuss Geisel; also known as Dr. Seuss. After years of looking out for ways to be introduced, he bumped into Dr. Seuss in a waiting room at a doctor's office and had a nice conversation. While he didn't land Geisel as a client, he likely would not have recognized him unless he kept his "ideal prospect" list.

LinkedIn allows you to be ruthless in identifying your perfect target client through the information available on the site and its search capabilities. Once you find someone you want to meet, LinkedIn automatically shows you a list of people in your network that can introduce you. Finding qualified prospects and asking for an introduction can be done from home in your slippers, instead of spending hours wasting time at networking events.

The first step is to create a list of traits for prospects that you want to meet, including:

- Their industry

- Their company

- Job title

- Location

- Alma Mater

- Charities and passions

- Hobbies

Each of these characteristics is searchable using LinkedIn advanced searches. With your list in hand, log in to LinkedIn to identify who you want to meet.

# Advanced Search

To translate your list of ideal prospect characteristics into a list of people you want to meet, we'll use the free LinkedIn Advanced Search feature. To do an advanced search, navigate to the very top of the page, next to the search bar, and click "Advanced."

| ≡ ▾ | Search for people, jobs, companies, and more... | 🔍 Advanced |

This will bring up the "Advanced Search" window, where you can search by:

1. Keyword (hobbies, passions, charities)

2. First Name

3. Last Name

4. Job Title

5. Company

6. School

7. Location

8. Industry

9. Non-Profit Interests

10. Years of Experience

11. Seniority Level

12. Company Size

The keyword search will scan their whole profile, including their headline. This is a good place to use search terms to target business owners with "CEO," "Founder," or "Owner." You could search for retirees with a keyword search for "Retired" or "Ret." for military retirees. Another option is to find IRA rollover money in motion through targeting job seekers with "Seeking," "Transitioning," or "Candidate" as a search term.

The possibilities are endless for creating custom advanced searches. Creative examples include:

- Qualcomm engineers who live within 10 miles of my office.

- Software industry business owners who like hunting.

- Biotech executives who are passionate about education.

- CEOs from University of Ohio who enjoy fine wine.

Be creative with your searches. One of my clients was having a golf clinic with a famous golf pro, so we used a custom search to find business owners in his area who golf. Another client was hosting a deep sea fishing trip, so we generated a list of entrepreneurs who enjoy sportfishing.

## Saved Searches

LinkedIn makes it so easy to identify folks you'd like to meet, it's not even funny. The saved search feature allows you to save up to three custom searches for free. Once you've created a custom search, look in the upper right corner of your results page to "save your search."

Better yet, you can set an alert to email you when new contacts come up for this search parameter. For example, if I work with Bay Area Surgeons, I can set a saved search to send me an email when a new surgeon moves to the Bay Area. Then, I can send a message to welcome them to the neighborhood and share how I may be able to help. Set up three saved searches today to get started. To access your saved searches, click on the gear button in the upper right hand corner in any search result page.

| Title | New | Alert | Created | |
|---|---|---|---|---|
| Executive Equestrians | - | Weekly | Jan 26, 2016 | |
| CEO's Who Golf | - | Weekly | Jan 28, 2015 | |

**Tip:** You can currently save up to 3 people searches to easily access from the results page.

# The Art of Asking for an Introduction

Research shows that the majority of affluent investors find their advisor through an introduction from someone they know and trust. So, once you've identified who you want to meet, the next step is to ask for an introduction from someone who already knows and trusts you. An existing client or member of your network is a great person to ask to make an introduction.

I know in my work doing Client Satisfaction Surveys for advisors that over 90% of clients often say they would recommend the advisor to a family member or friend. The problem is that when we ask them who they know that the advisor should contact, only a few clients provide names. Clients are willing to introduce you, but it's your responsibility to ask them for a specific introduction.

Keep in mind the golden rule for introductions; in-person is best, by phone is second best, and email is okay in a pinch. Also, remember the principle of reciprocity; don't ask a favor without doing something first for the person you're asking. Regular client meetings are the best opportunity to ask for an introduction in-person, after you've done something valuable for your client.

Before each regular client meeting, come up with a list of qualified prospects that your client is connected to on LinkedIn. I recommend preparing 3-5 names in advance of each meeting. Once you've completed your portfolio review and are wrapping up the meeting, ask the client if they're happy with the service you've provided. As soon as they've articulated to you (and to themselves) that they're happy with your work, ask them if they'd be willing to introduce you to someone they know that you may be able to help. Once they approve, bring up the first name on your list.

You can start the conversation by saying, "You know, I've been trying to get better at building my network on LinkedIn. Before our meeting, I took a look at your LinkedIn profile. I noticed that you're connected to John Peterson. As you know, I work with a lot of executives at your company like John."

The trick here is to gauge how well they know the person that you'd like to meet. If they're connected on LinkedIn but they don't actually know John, you're better off focusing on someone they know better. To gauge the connection, try asking "Is he a good guy?" or "How well do you know John?" and consider their response.

I find in my work with advisors that 75% of the time, the client will say "Sure, I'd be happy to make the introduction." About 25% of the time, they reveal that they don't know the prospect well, so you will want to move on to the next person on the list.

Once they've agreed to introduce you to the qualified prospect, you'll want to plan when the introduction will take place. Ask when they think they'll be seeing the person next. When they let you know, offer some polite accountability by saying "Great, enjoy your company picnic with John this weekend, and I will follow up with you Monday to hear how it went." That way, you can call them on Monday and remind them to make the introduction if they forgot.

As soon as you get into the habit on implementing this strategy, it becomes automatic and foolproof. Not every introduction will end in meeting with the prospect, but you will get an opportunity to explain who you are and how you may be able to help, allowing them to keep you in mind and potentially refer business in the future.

By consistently identifying who you want to meet and asking for the introduction, you can generate referrals to qualified prospects on a regular basis. In the next chapter, we'll review how to leverage custom content to target your target prospects and establish yourself as a subject matter expert.

# CHAPTER 5

# Content Marketing on LinkedIn

In the early days of LinkedIn, content marketing didn't have much of a place on the platform because LinkedIn was more of a Rolodex of contacts. However, with the introduction of the LinkedIn publishing platform, content is now king. If you embrace the publishing capabilities, you will get excellent exposure because:

- The average LinkedIn user spends 17 minutes per month on the site

- Over 80% of LinkedIn content is generated by the top 10% of users

I've built my own firm almost exclusively by creating weekly LinkedIn publications, and in my experience with advisors, about half of their total inbound marketing leads (leads approaching you, as opposed to you approaching them) come from the strategy I'm about to show you. The other half come from email marketing and other social platforms.

If you fully execute the steps in the last chapter and the steps in this chapter, I would venture to guess that 60% of your new clients will come from the last chapter's strategies, and 40% from content marketing strategies. What's more, your content strategy will help support your referral process, so it's important to do both concurrently.

# What is Content Marketing?

Content marketing uses the creation and distribution of content to earn the attention of prospects. Once you have their attention, they get to know you better and take the next step toward working with you. If you want to learn everything there is to know about content marketing, read *Content, Inc.* by Joe Pulizzi, which is a great resource with a menagerie of business examples.

You've likely been the target of content marketing from companies sending you eBooks, white papers, podcasts, and more. The goals of content marketing are to:

1. Earn the attention of prospects

2. Show them what you do and how you can help

3. Position yourself as a subject matter expert

4. Stay on top of mind

5. Start a conversation

6. Drive traffic to your LinkedIn profile or website

The strategy can be effective with general or "canned content," but is most effective when the content created is specialized and unique. You may be using a form of content marketing today if you're sending out market commentaries, videos, or other third party produced content to stay on top of mind. However, there has been a backlash against generic content in recent years, as we all tire of the noise.

Have you received an obviously mass-produced health or lifestyle article from your real estate agent or dentist? That type of content is annoying, because if you wanted to learn about the "Top Ten Vacation Spots in Europe," you would Google it yourself. Effective content marketing uses custom, original content that provides value specifically to your target demographic.

**Instead of:**
Ten Retirement Planning Mistakes

**Try:**
How to Maximize Your General Electric Benefits Package

**Instead of:**
Three Reasons to Use a Financial Advisor

**Try:**
Why I Became a Wealth Advisor to Single Women

**Instead of:**
Ten Keys to Investing

**Try:**
What Should You Do After Last Week's Stock Market Decline?

People in your network don't want to be bombarded with generic content, but they are interested in reading your expert opinion and insights on a timely topic. High-quality custom content addresses this need.

## Answer Your Prospects' Most Pressing Questions

Content marketing, in general, is aimed at helping people find you when they need you most. One direct way to do this is to answer the questions they are likely to type into Google. Oftentimes, I work with advisors to create posts that are the only answer available on Google for a common question their clients and prospects ask.

My Dad works with researchers and scientists at UC San Diego, where employees have both a 457 and a 403(b) plan to choose from. He is commonly asked what the difference is, so we created a blog post titled "What is the Difference Between the UC San Diego 457 and 403(b) Plans?" and another on "Making the Most of Your UC San Diego Employee Benefits." Posts like these are likely to be shared among groups of employees and between your clients and their coworkers, fostering referrals.

Another advisor I work with serves widowed and divorced spouses, so we created a series of posts on "The First Financial Steps to Take When Widowed," and "Five Financial Mistakes Widows Should Avoid." Posts like these are effective in helping prospects who were referred to your website or

LinkedIn profile get comfortable with your experience and expertise before they decide to make an appointment.

## Content Marketing on LinkedIn

You may not be aware of the three main ways to share information on Linkedin:

1. As a status update, which appears in the newsfeed of your connections

2. As a publication, which notifies all of your connections that you've published a post and permanently resides on your profile

3. Sharing your publications or updates within your LinkedIn groups

Because there are benefits to each avenue of sharing content, I recommend all three. Each time you create a post, you'll want to publish as a publication, share that publication within all of your groups, and share the publication as an update (more on that in the next chapter).

Since you've taken the time to create the content and get it approved by compliance, you should also publish to your website as a blog post, then send an email to your contacts directing them to the blog post. Then, you can share the blog post on LinkedIn to drive traffic back to your website. It's all about cross-pollination of your website and social profiles.

If you want to really maximize exposure for each piece of content you create, you can also build automated email workflows so that when a new contact signs up for your newsletter, they'll get an automatic campaign of emails showcasing the best content you've created. That's a great strategy, but it's the subject of another book.

Speaking of books, once you've been blogging regularly for a year or more, you will likely have enough content to publish a book! This can be a great marketing move to gain speaking engagements and position yourself as an expert. But for now, let's discuss how to create effective content.

# Creating Content

Top advisors spend significant portions of their work hours creating their own custom content. Michael Kitces, who is often ranked as the most social media savvy advisor in the US, spends a full 20% of his week writing for his blog. His content marketing strategy has helped grow his firm, Pinnacle Advisory Group, to over $1.8 billion in AUM. He is also an author, speaker, and frequently appears in the media.

However, if you don't have time or don't enjoy creating your own content, it's perfectly okay to outsource the job. Be sure that whoever creates your content keeps true to your opinions, insights, and philosophies. In my firm, the bread and butter of our work is creating and deploying custom content for top advisors. This comes in the form of blog posts, LinkedIn publications, eBooks, whitepapers, and email marketing. By outsourcing the job, they are able to take marketing off their plate and focus on what they do best.

If you know that you will not create content on a consistent basis, skip this section and outsource the task. It's more important to get the job done than to do it yourself. Although I create my own original content each week, I outsource the deployment of it because I know I don't enjoy the task and I'm likely to procrastinate.

If you happen to be a proficient writer or speaker, creating your own content can put you way ahead of the competition. Be sure to commit to a schedule (I recommend at least every other week) and put aside time make it happen.

## First, Get Clear on Your Niche

Who do you serve and how do you help them? Each piece of content should reiterate this point, no matter the subject of the blog post. Every time someone engages with a piece of content, we want to make sure to remind them that you are the go-to resource for your main thing.

# Choose Your Weapon: Types of Content

Advisors getting started with their content marketing strategy often get hung up on which type of content they should be creating. I recommend choosing whichever type is the easiest for you to create, so that it happens on a consistent basis. However, you should try each of the following types of content to see which resonates best with your network:

- Blog Posts
- Videos
- Charts or Graphics
- Podcasts
- Newsletters
- Whitepapers
- eBooks
- Books

## Wait, What is Blogging?

"Blog" is short for "Weblog," which refers to a post or article that appears on a website. My 68-year-old Dad still won't refer to his blog as a "Blog" because he finds it too techy and futuristic. He prefers to call his posts "Articles," which happen to reside in the blog portion of his website. Don't let blogging make you uncomfortable; most of you have been blogging for years by writing articles, brochures, newsletters, and market commentaries.

The biggest misconception I find that advisors have about blogging is that bloggers *write about themselves*. Unfortunately, there are many boring bloggers out there who go on and on about themselves. But in marketing, a blog should be *sharing your opinion on a topic that matters to your audience*.

People are interested in your expertise, insight, and opinions on topics they care about. You'll want to weave in stories, but the blog isn't about you, it's about them (your reader).

"Blog posts" or pieces of content can be however long and complex or short and sweet that you want to make them. I've created successful posts for advisors including:

- Articles
- Audio recordings
- Interviews with experts
- Charts or photos with a caption
- Short stories
- Polls or surveys

In my own firm, through trial and error, I've found that my network enjoys consuming marketing blog posts with data and examples as well as videos. I produce two articles and two videos each month that you can find on my LinkedIn profile under "Publications."

## Blogging and SEO

The content marketers of the world will usually cite search engine optimization, or SEO, as a main benefit of blogging. Blogging does improve the SEO for your website and LinkedIn profile by:

1. Keeping them up-to-date
2. Including keywords
3. Increasing traffic

SEO is a complex and ever-changing topic, but the gist is that by improving SEO you help people find your website (and LinkedIn profile). You can improve your SEO by:

- Increasing traffic to your site
- Increasing the time each visitor stays on your site
- Increasing the "sharing" of content on your site

Because blogging accomplishes these three goals, it will improve the SEO for your site. In fact, with the recent release of Google's new search algorithm, there are no longer effective ways to pay your way to the top of the search results page. Instead, you'll want to focus on hitting the points listed above. However, because very few people are eager to give their life savings to an advisor they found on Google, SEO has limited efficacy for advisors seeking new clients.

## Choose a Topic

To get started on your blogging journey, it's helpful to keep a list of blog topic ideas. I keep a paper notebook and a note app on my phone where I jot down ideas as they come to me. To start out, spend 10 minutes writing down the most common questions clients and prospects ask you. These are great starting points that will be popular and valuable.

Next, write a list of challenges your clients face. Consider doing a survey to ask clients what they want you to cover on your blog. When you read an interesting article, consider tweaking to fit your specific niche. Instead of "Five Tips to Retire Early," write "Five Steps for Orthodontists to Retire Early."

Review any content you've created in the past and do more of the most popular articles or web pages. If you read an interesting book, write a book review. Interview economists or thought leaders. Write about the conferences and webinars you attend.

## Blog Topic Generator

Still stuck? Use a blog topic generator! Hubspot has a handy free tool that will suggest blog posts with titles that are designed to do well on social media. It's easy and fun to use. Just enter three nouns and they deliver a month's worth of blog topics.

When I enter: "financial advisors" and "LinkedIn," the Hubspot blog topic generator suggests:

- 5 Tools Advisors Should be Using on LinkedIn

- 20 Myths About Financial Advisors

- What Will Financial Advisors Be Like In 100 Years?

- 14 Common Misconceptions About LinkedIn for Financial Advisors

Try out the tool at www.hubspot.com/blog-topic-generator#.

## LinkedIn Pulse Topic Generator

LinkedIn itself also has a blog topic generator, which is purportedly customized for topics your network will find compelling. To see their suggestions, login to LinkedIn and click on "Publish a Post". Then, in the upper left of your screen under "Writing Ideas" are five custom suggestions.

Here are some LinkedIn suggestions for one of my advisor clients:

- Should the Fed Raise, Lower or Hold?

- How is the Volatile Stock Market Going to Impact Your Business?

You could certainly take these ideas and make them more specific to add more value for your target market, "How is the Volatile Stock Market Going to Impact San Diego Biotech Companies?"

## Try an Overlap Post

Overlap posts cover topics where your interests overlap with the interests of your audience. I recommend choosing an overlap topic for every fourth post to keep your blog personal, unique, and fresh. Some of my top blog posts of all time have been overlap posts, including:

1. What is Harry Markowitz Doing Today?

2. How Much Travel is Too Much?

3. What Really Happens at a Tony Robbins Event?

4. Why I Work With Financial Advisors

# The Most Important Blog Post You'll Write All Year

There's one quick and easy blog post you can write that typically gets twice as many views as any other type: explaining why you do what you do. The concept is highlighted in Simon Sinek's book, Start with Why, and you can watch a short video that sums up the book on YouTube. We also reviewed how to "Start with Why" in Chapter 2 to write your profile. Even if you have your story included in your profile, take a few minutes to create a stand-alone blog post titled "Why I Became a Financial Advisor."

Answer these questions to start writing:

- How did you view money as a child?
- Who has been your financial or business mentor?
- Why do you come to work each day?
- What's the most difficult part of your job?
- Why is the most fulfilling part about your job?

Here's one of my favorite "Start With Why" blog posts:

*I became a Certified Divorce Financial Analyst to help my clients get a fair and equitable divorce settlement. Growing up, I saw that my mother was financially and emotionally dependent on my father. When they divorced, it was heartbreaking to see what she went through to pick up the pieces and put her life back together. I'm passionate about helping people who are going through that transition. I truly enjoy my work and know that I am making a difference in my clients' lives.*

*I work hard every day to understand what my clients need most during their divorce. It's my goal to provide true value to the settlement process, not just gather assets to manage. Through hard work, I know that we can get to a fair and equitable settlement that works not just today, but five and ten years down the road.*

*One of the benefits of working with a Certified Divorce Financial Analyst is that we are able to use tools like forensic accounting, lifestyle analysis, and business valuation to help facilitate settlements that may otherwise go to court.*

*Attorneys focus on the law, but they often lack expertise on the financial piece of the puzzle. I am able to provide a thorough analysis and testify as an expert witness in cases. Attorneys who have worked with me before know that the numbers I provide are accurate, which helps to shorten the timeframe and the cost of the settlement.*

*One of the hardest parts of my job is when I see clients who have already completed their settlements and realize that there are mistakes, but there's nothing we can do after-the-fact. It's so important to do the job right because the majority of my clients rely on this settlement for the rest of their lives.*

*My job is fulfilling because I am able to make a huge difference in someone's financial stability during a difficult time. The majority of my clients rely on this settlement for their entire financial future. What they get during this process is everything to them, and that's what drives me to do my best.*

## Ready, Set, Write!

A great idea for a blog post is nothing if you don't make it happen. My metaphor for writing is moving a pile of bricks from one side of a room to another. There are no shortcuts. You may find that you're inspired and in the zone and you write quickly one day, but some days those bricks feel extra heavy. Coffee helps.

I write in three stages to make the process easy and efficient:

1. First, I create a quick outline of the ideas I want to cover

2. Next, I type all of my thoughts as fast as I can, focusing on the logic of ideas, not the choice in words, spelling, or punctuation

3. Finally, I go back and adjust the prose, word choice, and sentence structure to improve readability

Lastly, I run each of my blog posts through an online grammar editor called Grammarly. It's free and it will correct most grammar, spelling and punctuation errors. It's also handy because if you double click on a word, it automatically provides you with synonyms, which is nice when you've repeated a word one too many times.

# How to Structure Your Blog Posts

Writing for the Internet is different from writing for fiction, the newspaper, academia, or a book. The readers on the Internet like short paragraphs and subheadings. This may be due to difficulty reading large text blocks on a computer screen. One reason it is important to add subheadings is that Google gives hierarchical weight to the keywords in your title and headlines. Try to add 2-3 subheadings per post.

Here's the basic blog structure I recommend:

## A Catchy Headline with Relevant Keywords

Did you know the first sentence of your blog post may be the most influential? It's entirely possible, which is why you should start each post with a "hook" to capture interest. Then, add some data to legitimize your stance, because research shows that 56% of readers attribute credibility to writers who cite data from trustworthy sources (The Onion).

*Next, you should tell your readers about the background of the issue and how it may impact them. This is known in marketing as "stating the problem." If you don't state the problem in a compelling way, no one will read your blog posts. If no one reads your blog post, all of your effort goes to waste and your business may soon flounder.*

## Does Your Blog Post Have a Subheading?

*Subheadings are important for SEO and to help guide the reader through your logic. Writing subheadings in the form of a question can help keep your reader engaged. Once you've explained the idea highlighted in your subheading, transition on to the next issue.*

## Offer An Attractive Alternative

*If you've properly made your reader aware of the problem and how it affects them, you'll want to offer a solution to take away the fear you've created. By doing this, your blog posts will make them feel warm and fuzzy, and they'll want to read more of your writing. When they read your writing on a regular basis, they will trust you and be more likely to do business with you. As a result, your business will surely flourish.*

*You can repeat the Subheading and Paragraph structure until you've come to your conclusion. Then, remember in the beginning of this fake article when we discussed adding third party data to increase credibility? You'll want to relate back to the hook and consider adding another piece of data, but be sure to cite your proper sources. Abraham Lincoln hit this point home in 1864 when he said, "The problem with quotes you find on the internet is that they're not always true."*

*Lastly, you'll want to add a call to action to invite the reader to take the next step, then an "About the Author" section to remind them exactly who you are, what you do, and how you can help. We'll go over this in the next section.*

If that faux post was too abstract for your taste, here's an example of a real life blog post with good "bones":

## Last Chance to File and Suspend to Maximize Social Security Benefits

*As you read on our blog in October, the last-minute budget and debt ceiling deal that the House and Senate passed will make significant changes to Social Security benefits. In an effort to decrease spending, Section 831 of the new budget slashes benefits for those using popular claiming strategies.*

*Some experts have estimated that the changes are equivalent to a decrease of $50,000 in lifetime benefits for many retirees. However, there is still time to take advantage of the file and suspend claiming strategy to maximize overall benefits for some who are close to retirement. If you or a loved one was born on or before May 1, 1950, it's important to take action now to evaluate available options.*

### History of the File and Suspend Strategy

*Fifteen years ago, the Senior Citizens Freedom to Work Act provided an option for "voluntary suspension" of benefits, allowing those taking Social Security benefits to stop receiving payments and earn delayed retirement credits, a practice which was termed "file and suspend." The new budget deal eliminates this option and removes some other popular claiming strategies.*

*The file and suspend claiming strategy will be eliminated as of May 1, 2016. The strategy has been popular for married couples, where one spouse can file and suspend benefits to allow the other spouse to begin claiming spousal benefits while the working spouse continues to accrue credits. The file and suspend changes also eliminate the ability to receive a lump sum for benefits that would have been receiving during the period of suspension if retirees decide to restart benefits.*

### Can You Still File and Suspend?

*There is still a chance for those approaching retirement to benefit from the file and suspend strategy, depending on their age. However, you must submit your request to file and suspend before April 30, 2016. Anyone who is 66 or older can file for benefits and immediately suspend them, allowing their benefits to earn additional credits, which may be worth 8% per year until age 70, which can increase their total benefit by up to 32%.*

*Social Security claiming strategies should always be reviewed with an experienced financial professional to optimize your total lifetime benefit. If you aren't sure whether the changes apply to you or have questions about your social security claiming strategy, call our office at 770.333.0113 x106 or email bill@ wealthandpension.com.*

## About Bill

*William "Bill" Kring is the founder of Wealth & Pension Services Group, Inc, an independent wealth management firm serving individuals and businesses near Atlanta, Georgia. As a twenty year financial veteran, Bill offers broad expertise in wealth management services including asset management, fiduciary consulting, retirement, trust and estate planning, as well as insurance and 401(k) plan services. In his past, he competed as a U.S. Cycling Federation class III rider in both road and track. To learn more about how Bill may be able to help, visit the Wealth & Pension website, connect with him on LinkedIn, call his office at 770.333.0113 x106 or email him anytime at bill@wealthandpension.com.*

## Adding Calls to Action

The aim of each piece of content is to get your prospect to take the next step. This could be small, from reading a related article, or big, like setting an appointment. Each piece of content should have a variety of "Calls to

Action" that allow the reader to take the next step that feels most comfortable for them.

Here are some examples of calls to action, from low stakes to high stakes:

Read a related article
Visit your website
Share a blog post with friends
Watch a video
Like your page on Facebook
Register for a webinar
Connect with you on LinkedIn
Download your eBook
Join your newsletter
Ask a question
Register for an event
Schedule an appointment

At the end of each piece of content you create, add this section to invite prospects to take the next step and remind them who you are and what you do. Here's an example from one of my blog posts on email marketing:

*Do you want to bring your email marketing up to speed? Visit my website to learn more about what I do or schedule a virtual meeting to discuss your email marketing. Not ready to double your leads with email marketing? Stay in touch by connecting with me on LinkedIn, visiting my blog, and registering for my courses.*

### About Claire Akin
*Claire Akin runs Indigo Marketing Agency a full-service marketing firm serving financial advisors. Claire is a former Investment Advisor Representative who holds her MBA in Marketing from the Rady School of Management at UC San Diego as well as a BA in Economics from UC Davis. It's her goal to help advisors leverage technology to grow their businesses.*

Here's an example from an advisor:
*To learn more about how we help CRNAs pursue financial freedom, visit*

*our website, sign up for our weekly CRNA financial tips, or download our book "The Wealthy CRNA." Feel free to ask a question anytime by emailing us at inquiry@crnafinancialplanning.com.*

### About Jeremy Stanley

*Jeremy Stanley is the founder of CRNA Financial Planning®. He has been providing advice and guidance for Certified Registered Nurse Anesthetists (CRNA) for over 20 years. As a CERTIFIED FINANCIAL PLANNER™, Jeremy has met rigorous certification and professional standards set by the CFP® Board. He is committed to adhering to the principles of integrity, objectivity, and professionalism. Jeremy is also the author of the book "The Wealthy CRNA," which lays out a foundational roadmap for CRNAs to help them plan their financial future.*

The call to action section should accompany the blog post on your website and on LinkedIn so that when you share either within groups, even people who are not connected to you can take the next step.

## Add a Graphic

According to marketing giant Hubspot, articles with images get 94% more total views than articles without images. I use Canva.com to create images for each of my posts for $1 each. The proper size for a LinkedIn publication graphic is 700 by 400 pixels. You'll want the image to be high resolution, but not too large that it takes a long time to load; about 40-50 KB is just right. High-quality images of people similar to your target audience are best. Don't spend too much time on the imagery, the most important thing is that your post has an image.

## Add Disclosures and Send Through Compliance

Because your LinkedIn publications will appear on their own without your website disclosures, you'll want to add disclosures to each post. Then, because the post will go out to the public, it will need to be approved by compliance in advance.

## Post to LinkedIn

Once your article is approved by compliance, it's time to post to LinkedIn. I recommend posting on the same day each week or every other week in the morning, say 8am. To publish your post:

1. Log in to LinkedIn

2. Click on "Publish Post"

3. Copy and Paste Your Headline into "Write Your Headline"

4. Copy and Paste Your Blog into the body of the post

5. Add three relevant tags (keywords for that post)

6. Upload your image

7. Hit "Publish"

This will notify everyone in your network that you've published a post and the article will reside permanently on your profile under "Publications." You will likely get a few likes, comments, and direct messages about your post.

## Share to Groups

To double the exposure for each post, it's important to share it within your groups. Remember, you should join up to the limit of 50 groups where your ideal prospects are likely to belong. There's a trick to sharing to all of your groups at once:

1. Go to your post by going to your profile, then clicking on "Posts"

2. Once you open the post you'd like to share, click on the little LinkedIn icon right under the headline

3. This will pop up the "Share News on LinkedIn" pop up box

4. Go ahead and uncheck "Share an Update" and check the box for "Share to Groups"

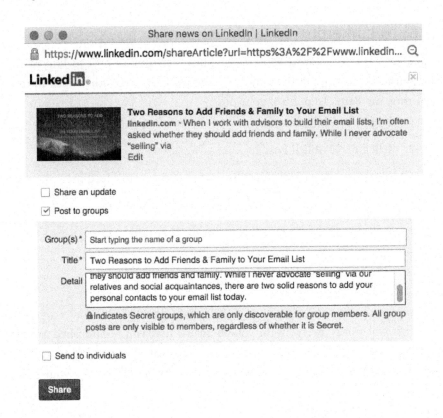

Then, fill in the headline and a teaser sentence or two of the article. Finally, type the first letter of each group name (I type A through Z in order) to bring up all of your groups. Once all of your groups are populated, click "Share." This will notify all group members (even those you aren't connected to) that you've published a post.

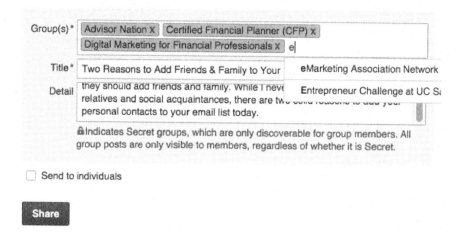

The LinkedIn default notification setting for groups is to receive a weekly digest email. If members of the group have not changed their settings, they'll receive an email notification of your post. It's almost like adding hundreds of people from your target audience to your email list!

The biggest challenge I see facing advisors who want to create a content marketing strategy is perfectionism. Don't let perfectionism keep you from deploying your content. Putting out a B+ post is much more effective than no post at all.

We know that content marketing works, but most advisors don't do it because it's hard work. Keep in mind that most new activities are difficult at first (running, tennis, guitar), but get easier with practice. Challenge yourself to publish LinkedIn blog posts every week for the next six months. I guarantee you'll expand your network, improve your referral pipeline, and generate new leads as a result.

# CHAPTER 6

# Tying it All Together & Advanced Techniques

N ow that you have an amazing profile, you're using LinkedIn to ask for introductions at every client meeting, and you're posting bi-weekly publications to stay top of mind as a subject matter expert, it's time to tie all of your marketing efforts together. The ongoing goals of your strategy are to:

- Keep growing your network

- Cross-pollinate between LinkedIn and other marketing efforts

- Get more exposure for each post

- Use advanced techniques when appropriate

There are a variety of upfront and continuing steps to help pursue these goals on a regular basis:

## Add Your Profile to Your Email Signature and Business Cards

First, I recommend adding a "Connect with me on LinkedIn" link to your email signature. This way, as you email back and forth with clients and colleagues, they'll be reminded to connect with you. LinkedIn provides "Badges" (little icons) for this purpose, but I prefer a simple hyperlink to avoid attaching an image to each email.

You may have noticed that when you email back and forth with folks who have images in their email signature, the images accumulate at the bottom of the email and start to add up. A simple "Connect with me on LinkedIn" hyperlinked to your profile will get the job done without adding an unneeded attachment to each email. Are you still using printed business cards? If so, next time you print business cards, add your LinkedIn profile URL so that folks you meet can connect with you.

## Invite the Audience to Connect When You Present

If you do any type of speaking engagements, be sure to list your profile URL on your final slide and ask the audience to connect to stay in touch. Remember when we created a vanity URL (www.linkedin.com/in/claireakin) so it's easy to type? List this on the screen so people can jot it down and send you an invitation. This way, when they have a question after the event, they can send you a quick message. They'll also see all of your updates and publications.

## Download the Mobile App

LinkedIn has a mobile app that allows you to send and receive messages via your smartphone, as well as browse your news feed. Download it through the app store and use it to stay connected on the go.

## Import Your Email List Twice a Year

In Chapter 3, we reviewed how to import all of your email addresses to connect with your contacts on LinkedIn. Because you're adding email addresses to your contact list all the time, you'll want to export those contacts to LinkedIn twice a year to add those connections.

*Here are the steps for reference:*
Start on LinkedIn by going to Connections, then "Add Connections." You can then connect an existing email account, such as Gmail, Hotmail, Yahoo, etc. However, for most advisors, this is not helpful because they are typically required to use compliance archived email servers. In these cases, you'll need to import your contacts.

To do this, the trick is to export your contacts from your customer relationship management (CRM) system or email server as an Excel spreadsheet or .CSV file. The process to do this is different for each email server or CRM, but it is typically a built-in functionality that isn't too difficult. If you do a quick Google search for the system you are using, you will find step-by-step directions. For Outlook 2010, here are the steps:

1. Open Outlook 2010 and click File > Options

2. When the Outlook Options window opens, click Advanced

3. In the Import and Export Wizard window, select the Export to a file option, then Next

4. In the File Type option, select Comma Separated Values (Windows) option to create a CSV file

If you have trouble, call tech support and they can walk you through the process. If you can't export as a .CSV file, that's no problem; just export as an Excel file, then open the spreadsheet in Excel. Click on File, then Export, and select ".CSV" to change the file type. Once you save the .CSV version of your spreadsheet, you can upload directly to LinkedIn by clicking on "Import File" in the "Add Connections" section.

Remember to import email addresses from your various systems, whether you have a CRM, email address book, financial planning software, email newsletter list, etc. By uploading as many of your contacts as you can, you'll maximize your network.

## Add Your Social Profiles to Your Website

Ask your website developer to add icons that link to your LinkedIn profile and any other social media sites to the top of your home page so people can connect with you that way. This is easy for them to do and is standard for website user experience, meaning site visitors expect to be able to find your profiles on your home and contact pages.

## Add Your Profiles to Your Email Templates

If you are using an email system like Constant Contact, Hubspot, MailChimp, or MarketingPro, remember to add your website and social media profiles there too, so everyone who is on your email list has a chance to connect with you. Most email platforms have built-in interfaces to add a "social bar." Here's what it looks like:

## Add Social Sharing to Each Page of Your Website

It's easy to have your web developer install "Social Sharing" software on your site so that visitors can share an article or blog post on LinkedIn, Facebook, Twitter, or by email with one click. I use a free software called SumoMe.com to accomplish this. All pages of my client's sites feature these share buttons so visitors can easily send posts to friends, family, and share with their network.

## Take the 2016 Marketing Challenge!

January 06, 2016 / Claire Akin

Will 2016 be a hit or a flop for your business? Like it or not, in marketing, you get out what you put in. Take the 2016 marketing challenge to invest in your business and grow your AUM this year! Watch this video to learn more.

## Always Hyperlink Your Name to Your LinkedIn Profile

In digital marketing, we're constantly trying to find ways to hyperlink pieces of text to drive traffic back to our websites. If one of our articles is published online, it's a tragic lost opportunity if the publication doesn't link to our site so readers can learn more about what we do.

You should always be thinking about ways to promote your website and your LinkedIn profile. Try adding a hyperlink to your name and website for your bio, any bylines in publications, or mentions in the news. Everywhere my name appears, I list it with built in links like this: Claire Akin (Link to LinkedIn Profile), MBA Indigo Marketing Agency (Link to Website). This makes it easy for folks to learn more about me and my company.

## Reuse Your Publications

Because you're spending time and energy creating insightful and targeted publications each month, you'll want to maximize their exposure. There are plenty of ways to do this, including:

- Publish to your website as a blog post

- Send an email to your newsletter list

- Print as a helpful handout for new clients or prospects

- Share as an email to answer frequently asked questions

- Pitch to relevant publications and local newspapers

- Consider paid placement of your articles in newspapers and magazines

One of my clients serves the affluent neighborhood of Rancho Santa Fe, California and successfully uses a paid placement of her articles in the local newspaper, positioning her as the go-to expert for wealthy women in the area. Another client works exclusively with CPAs, so he does a monthly ad in the most popular local CPA trade journal.

## Create Presentations from Your Posts

Once you've taken the time and thought to write articles and come up with charts and graphics on a topic, it's not too much more work to create a presentation. Consider using these presentations for client events, prospecting lunches, or webinars.

When I find that a blog post topic performs in the top 10%, I create a presentation from the article, shoot a video of the presentation, and add it to my "Courses" section of my website so visitors can watch it anytime. Be creative to get maximum mileage from your best content.

# Advanced Techniques

What would a book on LinkedIn be without discussing some of the advanced and paid features? I get a lot of questions from advisors on advanced techniques, but the truth is that 90% of your success on LinkedIn will come from strategically using the free features.

In 2014, LinkedIn and Guardian Life Insurance Company embarked on what was supposed to be a groundbreaking pilot program of financial professionals using LinkedIn Premium and Sales Navigator. Sales Navigator is a version of LinkedIn premium that "suggests" qualified leads for you based on a "sophisticated algorithm." The advisors in the program were coached to use all of the available features and had LinkedIn support along the way.

Did you hear about their explosive success? Me neither. The program was unenthusiastically summarized in a single article on LinkedIn's blog. *Forbes* featured a story of one Guardian advisor who "successfully leveraged his LinkedIn network to widen his reach, connect with high net worth prospects and identify more than 30 qualified prospects in just six months." But that advisor was not reported to actually bring in any new business and you and I both know you can use the free features we discussed in Chapter 4 to identify qualified prospects.

I've spent a lot of time piloting paid LinkedIn strategies with little success. This is because the paid features generally focus on allowing you to connect with folks who you don't know as well, which is where our success starts to break down. The strategies that I know to be effective rely on getting introductions from those who know and trust us, as well as helping others get to know us over time through content marketing. However, it's helpful to understand the advanced tools available.

## LinkedIn Premium

There are several versions of LinkedIn Premium, depending on if you're a job seeker, a sales rep, or an advertiser. LinkedIn Premium is a subscription-based service that "unlocks" special features on LinkedIn including:

- Enhanced profile (larger photo and headline)
- The ability to see who (outside your network) has viewed your profile
- Advanced search capabilities
- 25 InMail credits
- 25 Introduction request credits
- Up to 10 saved searches

The cost is $60 per month or $575 per year. The problem is that most of the features focus on connecting with those you don't already know, which isn't helpful in the referral process we've proven to be effective. Enhancing your profile could be cool, but it also may come off as a little sales-y. Following up with those who view your profile can seem creepy and the free feature already allows you to see who within your network has viewed your profile.

Advanced search capabilities are helpful, but probably not worth almost $600 per year. Introduction requests are not helpful for our purposes because we always try to ask in person, by phone, or by email in a pinch. Finally, unlocking more than the standard three saved searches can certainly be helpful if you are using them to identify who you want to be introduced to, so you will have to decide whether that convenience is worth $60 per month.

## InMail Messages

InMail Messages allow you to send a message to someone on LinkedIn who you are not connected to and the messages only "count" if the recipient responds. You must have a premium subscription to get InMail messages and the number provided each month depend on your subscription level.

I worked with one advisor who was adamant about using paid InMail messages to introduce himself to everyone who fit his prospect profile in his community. I'm always up for trying new strategies, so together we crafted a compelling message to introduce who he was and how he may be able to help and paid to send it to everyone in our target demographic. The results were lukewarm at best, with no concrete leads as a result.

InMail messages work much better for "Business to Business" marketing efforts. I have one third party administrator client who has been successful in reaching out to advisors on LinkedIn via InMail to set introduction appointments. I have another advisor who works exclusively with dentists and has used LinkedIn InMail to connect with administrators of Dental Schools to pitch teaching his course, "Business Fundamentals for Dentists."

I've also used InMail to connect with industry leaders and key influencers regarding this book and other efforts. If it makes sense for you to reach out to folks you don't know using InMail, knock yourself out, but don't get your hopes up for landing new advisory clients.

## LinkedIn Ads

If you are dying to pour some money into your LinkedIn efforts, I would first recommend increasing your content marketing, and then if there's money leftover, LinkedIn ads. There are a two main types of ads:

- Sponsored updates (to get more exposure for each post)
- Text ads (the ads that show up on the right panel of your LinkedIn screen)

The problem with paid ads in our industry is that there is a lot of competition from companies with deep pockets that drives up the price. The typical cost per click for an ad with "financial advisor" as the keywords is around $6. This means that you will pay $6 per person who clicks on the ad and goes to your website. I have not come across an advisor with a website that can convert at a high enough rate to make this cost worthwhile. We know that using a consistent content marketing strategy can get traffic to your website for less than $2 per visitor, so your marketing budget would be better spent creating and deploying more high-quality content.

However, increasing the reach of each post with a sponsored update can be an effective way to get more exposure for existing content. The problem is that you have to promote posts from your company page, not your profile, which isn't ideal for our purposes. We find that prospects want to do business with a person, not a corporate page. Once you create your company page and advertising account, you can select an existing post to "promote" to a targeted network of your choosing.

You'll select the location, industry, company size, job title, etc. (all of the same search parameters we reviewed in Chapter 4). However, one distinct advantage is that you can also target age and gender, which are missing from the general search features.

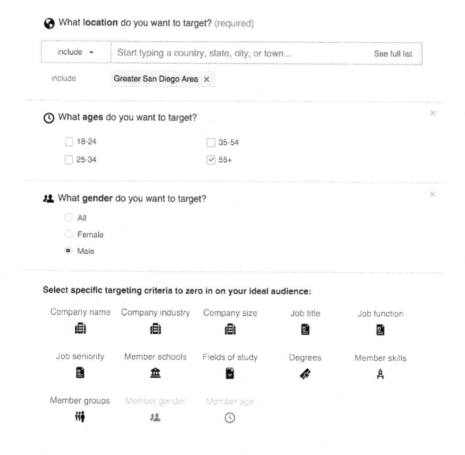

Once you target your audience, you'll set your budget. Again, the cost per click for LinkedIn campaigns typically provides a negative ROI for advisors. For each click to a blog post under a "paid campaign," LinkedIn suggests a cost per click of about $5.75.

Keep in mind, this is for a post from the advisor's company page, not their profile, which will not convert as effectively. In any case, you can set the cost per click maximum (if you set it too low, you won't get many clicks) or the daily budget.

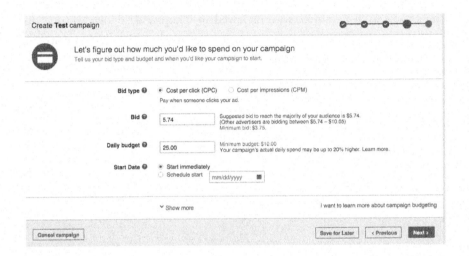

Once you've finalized your campaign, you can enter your credit card number and schedule the ad. If you decide to try out paid campaigns, please share your success with me, as I love to hear what is working and what's not. Paid ads can and do work more effectively for business to business advertising, so if you're promoting a service or an event to other professionals, ads may make more sense for you.

# The Future of LinkedIn

As a publicly traded company, LinkedIn has an obligation to its shareholders to generate revenue, yet most members pay nothing for the service. CEO Jeff Weiner envisions membership growing to over 3 billion users globally. Recruiters are the company's main source of revenue and that will likely continue into the future. However, be on the lookout for LinkedIn to come up with creative ways to offer you premium services for additional fees.

One recent advancement in the recruiting market was to allow passive job seekers, those who are not actively looking for a job but would move for the right offer, to privately identify themselves to recruiters. Advancements like this in the financial services industry are plausible and we know LinkedIn has directed resources towards creating a value-add solution for financial professionals.

Be on the lookout for LinkedIn asking you to "pay to play," especially if you are promoting a company page. Facebook has already altered their model so companies promoting their content must pay to "boost" their posts in order to reach a reasonable audience, so I see no reason that LinkedIn would not follow.

However, with most of the company's growth occurring overseas today, and most of its revenue from the employment market, financial advisors may be able to generate valuable referrals on LinkedIn while paying nothing for years to come.

## Stay In Touch and Up-to-Date

LinkedIn updates their software pretty regularly and their mobile app has undergone some significant changes in early 2016. Keep on top of any changes by logging in regularly and poking around. Don't get stressed out if new changes seem difficult to use or frustrating, the development team has a history of trying new things then reverting to the old methods if users don't like the updates.

Above all else, keep an optimistic attitude and have fun on social media. If you get stuck, ask your kids for help or simply Google what you're trying to accomplish. If you have questions, comments, or feedback, email me at claire@indigomarketingagency.com. If you found this book to be helpful, please leave a positive review on Amazon.com.

Join my newsletter and follow my blog for the latest updates and new strategies for advisors on LinkedIn. Ask your broker-dealer to have me present at your national conference and look out for an updated edition of this book for 2017!

# About the Author

Claire Akin runs Indigo Marketing Agency, a full-service marketing firm serving a handful of top financial advisors. She is an author, speaker, and expert in content marketing and social media. Claire is a former Investment Advisor Representative who holds her MBA in Marketing from the Rady School of Management at UC San Diego as well as a BA in Economics from UC Davis.

It's her goal to help advisors leverage marketing to grow their businesses. She lives in San Diego with her toxicologist husband (Josh), their dog (Wally), and their two American Paint Horses (Harley and Brandy). She has climbed Mt. Whitney three times and won a blue ribbon at the Del Mar Fair for her "Happy Hiker" trail mix.

CPSIA information can be obtained at www.ICGtesting.com
Printed in the USA
BVOW06s2235160716

455834BV00022B/234/P